CELEBRATING THE SACRED IN MINISTRY

THE RITES, RITUALS, ORDINANCES, AND PRAYERS AND BLESSINGS OF THE CHURCH

Dr. Lee Ann B. Marino, Ph.D., D.Min., D.D.

CELEBRATING THE SACRED IN MINISTRY

THE RITES, RITUALS, ORDINANCES, AND PRAYERS AND BLESSINGS OF THE CHURCH

Dr. Lee Ann B. Marino, Ph.D., D.Min., D.D.

Published by:
APOSTOLIC UNIVERSITY PRESS
www.apostolicuniversity.org

Unless otherwise noted, all Scriptures taken from the King James Version of the Holy Bible, Public domain.

Passages marked NIV are taken from the Holy Bible, New International Version ®, NIV® (1984),
Copyright © 1973, 1978, 1984, 2011 by Biblica, Inc.™
Used by permission of Zondervan.
All rights reserved worldwide.

Scriptures marked "CEB" taken from the Common English Bible®, CEB®
Copyright © 2010, 2011 by Common English Bible.™ Used by permission.
All rights reserved worldwide.

Scriptures marked "AMPC" taken from The Amplified® Bible, Classic Edition
Copyright © 1954, 1958, 1962, 1964, 1965, 1987 by The Lockman Foundation.
Used by permission. (www.Lockman.org)

Photos appearing in this book are all in the public domain or the design of the author.

ISBN: 1-940197-44-9
13-Digit: 978-1-940197-44-9

Printed in the United States of America.

In the west, the place of seeing
There is born a vision new:
Of the Servant of the Servants
Who proclaimed a Gospel true.
Let the creatures of creation
Echo back creation's prayer
Let the Spirit now breathe through us
And restore the sacred there.
- Marty Haugen, *Song At The Center*

It is the LORD of heavenly forces whom you should hold sacred, whom you should fear, and whom you should hold in awe…Bind up the testimony; seal up the teaching among my disciples. I will wait for the LORD, Who has hidden His face from the house of Jacob, and I will hope in God. Look! I and the children the LORD gave me are signs and wonders in Israel from the LORD of heavenly forces, who lives on Mount Zion.
- Isaiah 8:13,16-17 (CEB)

TABLE OF CONTENTS

INTRODUCTION

HONORING THE SACRED

WHEN I did my original book, *Rites, Rituals, And Ordinances: Celebrating The Sacred In Ministry*, I sought to establish the necessary "how-to" structure that many lack when it comes to formal ceremonies and occasions. It was my desire to give the necessary freedom to meet the needs that are present that time while giving a guide, or format, by which to do what needs doing. The process was most exciting to me, as I was able to incorporate several different writings I'd had around for ages about baptism, communion, ordination, and consecration while learning and growing through the insights needed to put the book into print. It was both an enlightening and educating journey in a practical sense.

In a deeper sense, the book served to me as a deep realization of how much I love the things of God and desire to honor the sacred in my life and ministry. If there is one thing I often miss and do not find in many churches today, it is the concept of the sacred. Lost amidst entertainment, light shows, proper teaching, and concept of reverence, we find the meeting place of multiple generations, none of whom understand the concept of "holy ground." As a result, we see a total lack of unity and cohesiveness when it comes to honoring the passages of God's sacred presence within our lives. Today we see a wide variety of ceremonies: everything ranging from the very elaborate to the very simple. Some modern groups believe in the total absence of anything related to ceremonies and rites, and others believe the entire validity of one's faith experience depends on these different rituals and rites. Some reject any form of blessing or prayer that is written down, and others reject any prayer that is spontaneous. No matter what someone believes about rituals, rites, and ordinances, there is only one word to describe the church's position on them: confused. In its struggle for truth in modern times, the church has succumbed to the dangerous temptation in embracing extreme positions, ignoring facts, and overlooking the relevance of the Word on matters of rites and rituals.

I have also observed that we don't understand nor have the needed reverence when it comes to prayers and blessings in our work. We understand the need to pray spontaneously, but the condition of our emotional states, mental driftings, and spiritual angst often make it so we don't know what to pray or how to celebrate someone else or acknowledge a ceremony in the form of prayer. Public prayer sometimes takes different forms than our private prayers, and knowing how to pray both in formal and informal settings is a big part of ministry work.

When we divorce ourselves from God's ordered rites, rituals, and ordinances, we divorce ourselves from God's purpose for us. When we distance ourselves from prayer and being able to speak forth words of comfort, praise, or blessing, It's essential for the minister of God to embrace the important symbolism present in rites, rituals, ordinances, and the important words echoed in prayer and blessing. These important aspects of the believer's journey celebrate each step of God's presence in life and acknowledge different life passages within the faith. As we see God present in these different stages, we recognize the spiritual and the sacred aren't quite as distant, nor as far away, as we might often think. Rites, rituals, and ordinances call to mind the life, death, and resurrection of our Lord, our leaders and heroes in the faith, celebrate the things God continues to do in His people today, and their choices, calls, and vocations in life. Prayers and blessings prove that communication is as close as when we call out to our Lord, and we know that He will bless us within His great mercy and love.

The ordained minister should be keenly aware of the relevance in celebrating rites, rituals, and ordinances and of praying and blessing in public assembly. As leaders, we are called to teach on, educate about, and officiate for these monumental events in people's lives. That means that we ourselves should learn of them and have received those applicable to us, our call, and our walk. It is wrong to think these rites, rituals, and ordinances can be done away with because these, in essence, are the "holidays" and celebrations specifically for the believer. Rather than play them down, we should raise them up, along with their powerful symbolism, uniqueness (such as these are different, special, and unique from those found in any other belief system worldwide), and sacred holiness.

In this book we will examine ten different rites, rituals, and ordinances for the church: Ordination, Appointments, Weddings, Funerals, Presentations/Dedications, Consecrations, Graduation Ceremonies and Sacred Assemblies, Anointing, Water Baptism, and Holy Communion. Within each we will look at the relevance and significance behind them, their importance, proper form, formula, and keys to working with individuals to make their ceremonies special and meaningful as a lasting remembrance of God's work within them. In the last section of this updated version, I am including a section of prayers and blessings for the church. I by no means attempt to imply that spontaneous prayer is irrelevant for the church; not in the least. These prayers and blessings exist for those moments when one is unsure of what to say or wants some basic inspiration to get started in those ceremonial or public moments.

We all know there are ministers today who never see the outside of a pulpit and who believe ministry is all about church preaching. It is not uncommon to meet ministers with no ministry experience aside from preaching. I am not one of these ministers, and I do not train nor encourage ministers to see ministry in such a limited and Being a minister of God is about far more than just preaching: it is about serving. Part of ministry service is administering the rites, rituals, and ordinances of the Lord and praying for and on behalf of God's people. In this manual, we will learn about these rites, how to perform them, how to conduct ourselves, and why these various rites, rituals, ordinances, and prayers are so essential. These works are not just essential to the recipient, but to the leader as well because they remind us of the continual work and process God does within each and every one of us as we go through our walk of faith with Him.

SECTION I

RITES

075229

AN ORDINATION IN AUSTRALIA

CHAPTER ONE

ORDINATION

And He ordained twelve, that they should be with Him,
and that He might send them forth to preach,
And to have power to heal sicknesses, and to cast out devils.
- Mark 3:14-15

WHAT IS ORDINATION?

Ye have not chosen Me, but I have chosen you, and ordained you, that ye should go and bring forth fruit,
and that your fruit should remain: that whatsoever ye shall ask of the Father in My Name, He may give it you.
- John 15:16

Ordination is the Biblical rite by which leaders are commissioned and purposed for ministry. The term "ordination" is used to indicate a leader's call is ordered of God and that their steps in ministry are ordered of God. True ordination confirms what God has put into place within a person's life, celebrates it, acknowledges it, and provides legal documentation of it. Overall, ordination is the celebration of God's call to leadership in one's life.

SHOULD WE DO ORDINATIONS?

And as they went through the cities, they delivered them the decrees for to keep,
that were ordained of the apostles and elders which were at Jerusalem.
- Acts 16:4

Nowadays ordinations seem to be found everywhere. Ordination used to follow a seminary education, Bible college education, or denominational training. People went to receive training from the organization they desired to acknowledge them as ministers and to affirm their call to ministry, and this came through the process of ordination. Now ordinations are found through internet sites, can be purchased for a price, and are often given out for no other purpose than so someone can perform their friend's wedding. We also see examples of churches that otherwise might seem to be following proper procedure or protocol, handing out papers like they are candy. The reason for this is simple: there is a great push to see "leaders" come out of churches, especially if the leader claims to be an apostle or a prophet. The more people who receive ordination credentials, the more "legitimate" a ministry seems to others looking in from the outside. Of course, such assertions are absurd, but they have led to a rush of individuals who don't understand what ordination is or how important it is for an individual to be licensed and ordained to ministry. As a result, ministries feel the push to "prove" themselves to others by ordaining others, whether or not those people are qualified to be ordained. The order of ordination is lost in modern strides to make ministry something that can be bought or handed off with a piece of paper. In response to modern desecrations of ordination, there are many churches now downplaying the relevance in ordination, stating a call is between a person and God, and no longer performing ordinations.

It is a misnomer to believe a ministry call is between a person and God. It is true that this is where a call begins, but a call to ministry is just as much for the church as it is for the individual who receives it. If our call is not recognized by both God and by people (maybe not every person, and certainly not every ministry, but at least a ministry group), then our ministry call is invalid. The Word tells us that Jesus gave gifts unto men, and those gifts are manifest in the five-fold ministry (Ephesians 4:8-15). This means ministry is between the individual and God, and is also between the individual and the church. Ordination is the symbol of this relationship between the minister and the church. The church leaders and the church body are affirming the leadership call, the ordered steps of God's leader and their purpose within the body.

We cannot ignore the bridge between ministry and the church. There is no question that the world is out of control and spinning faster and faster all the time. The world's disorder, however, does not give us the right to be disordered within and among ourselves. Ordination is still an acknowledgement that must go forth when someone is called to ministry.

We must also acknowledge that whether we want to deal with it or not, ordination has a legal component to it as well. To this end, we recognize spiritual and academic preparations for ordination to be valid among leadership within the church. Ordination opens the door for a minister to perform legally valid baptisms, weddings, funerals, communion services, ordinations (as applicable), and to operate in the fullness of ministry in the eyes of the law.

The last reason why ordination remains important is spiritual in nature. The laying on of hands, the spiritual words and empowerment, and the prayers spiritually prepare the person for all that lies ahead of them in ministry.

God's order for ministry has not changed. God's ordering of ordination has not changed. We, as the church, must still encourage and support the rite of ordination.

THE OFFICES OF ORDINATION

And He gave some, apostles; and some, prophets; and some, evangelists; and some, pastors and teachers.
- Ephesians 4:11

One of the biggest questions many have when it comes to ordination is who gets ordained? In a world full of titles, which ones reflect a genuine ordination? The answers to these two questions overlap in terms of technicality and in the strictest definitions of who should be ordained and who should not. The reality is, however, that acknowledgements of ordination technically go far beyond the immediacies of Christianity, and that when it comes to what someone calls themselves, different groups accept different credentials and different titles. What I am to present here is what is in alignment with the law and the Scriptures, which means that you may meet people who acknowledge different levels of ordination or different combinations of ordination credentials. In terms of the strictest definition of ordination papers that are acknowledged legally and spiritually, the following are the appropriate offices for ordination:

- **Minister** – The term "minister" means "servant," and is typically applied to anyone in the five-fold and to anyone who is serving in ministry in some capacity. This means that any apostle, prophet, evangelist, pastor, or teacher is, from a legal and spiritual capacity, a minister. The term is also used to apply in a general sense to people who may be ordained without falling into the category of a specific office. "Minister" may indicate someone is within a special sort of service within their church or ministry, is a chaplain or minister who works in a secular area, someone who serves in the appointment ministries and holds credentials for the sake of preparedness or ministerial purpose, an individual who holds license to preach, or someone who works in the social gospel arena and needs papers for the different works they may do in that ministry.

In my book, *Touching The Church In Eternity: A Journey Through The Book Of Ephesians* (Righteous Pen Publications, 2016) I define the five-fold ministry offices as follows:

- **Apostle** – Meaning, "one who is sent." The primary purpose of the apostle is to go forth with the mysteries of God in order to establish a proper foundation for the growth and development of the church (1 Corinthians 4:1-2). This means that the apostle works to implement structure in each church. They teach, train, establish, and install leaders in every congregation (Acts 2:42, 1 Corinthians 4:17, 1 Corinthians 12:28, Philippians 2:22, 1 Timothy 1:18). Some believe that apostles only have authority if they establish a congregation themselves, but we can see from the New Testament that this perspective is incorrect (Revelation 1:4). Apostles are universal authorities, which means that they have been given authority in the universal church, and do have that anywhere they go (whether or not it is wise to exercise such authority is a discernment call) (Ephesians 2:20). The apostle serves as God's ambassador, representing the cause of the Gospel wherever they go. They are the administrators of the church, insuring that the leaders of the church are properly equipped for their work, and that each church lacks nothing in substantial teaching and spiritual understanding (1 Timothy 4:1-9, 1 Timothy 5:22, 2 Timothy 1:6, Hebrews 6:2, 2 Peter 1:12-21, 2 Peter 2:1-22).

- **Prophet** – Meaning "one who speaks for or discerns the will of God." The work of the prophets has been seen from old, especially in the work of the Old Testament. The basic purpose of a prophet is to deliver God's message to His people and to explain and discern matters that relate to prophecy (Revelation 10:9-11). As the apostle brings structure to the church, the prophet brings the voice of God to it, setting a certain level of order and authority in the church (Amos 3:7, 1 Corinthians 14:36-40, Ephesians 3:5). Rather than being administrative, the prophet is mystical, bringing a spiritual quality and purpose to all that the church does (Ezekiel 2:1-10, Hosea 12:10). In like kind, the prophet trains other prophets and works to teach that necessary intimacy with God required for a prophet to know the voice of God as they go through different changes, seasons, and times in their own lives (1 Samuel 19:18-24). Like the apostle, the prophet is also a universal authority, and operates such with discernment (Ephesians 2:19-21). Along with that discernment, the prophet is there to discern the spirits present within people and within the church (1 Corinthians 14:31-32, 1 John 4:1-3).

- **Evangelist** – Meaning "Christ-bearer." The evangelist's work is often distorted in the church today, as the first "rung" up the five-fold ministry ladder, and the evangelist is considered to be someone who travels around to different churches to preach. If we look at the work of the evangelist in the New Testament, assigning such work to the evangelist is incorrect (although there is nothing wrong with an evangelist traveling to different churches and preaching). They are not apostles even though they do preach beyond the borders of local churches, thus clarifying that the evangelist's office has its own work and purpose. Evangelists are called to carry the Gospel to the world, especially to the non-believer or the individual who is in a state of separation from God (Acts 8:5-6, Acts 8:27-40). The evangelist is in the category of having authority with a universal scope, without formalized church authority (meaning they are not superior to universal or local authorities, but operate a position parallel to such that relates to the growth and management of the church) (Isaiah 61:1-3). They are independent, but still accountable to the church for what they teach, for which they have been thoroughly equipped for their ministry (2 Timothy 4:5).

- **Pastor** – Meaning "shepherd." The work of the pastoral office was prophesied by the Prophet Jeremiah (Jeremiah 3:15-16), and the reason we do not have a lot of New Testament references for the pastor is because the first Christians would have understood the office of the pastor to relate back to Jeremiah's prophecy. Just like the literal shepherds, pastors of the church have the job of spiritually feeding and caring for the flock entrusted to them, as well as ensuring that the flock remains together (Psalm 23:1-6, Jeremiah 12:10-17). This means that the majority of people pastors will work with are not leaders, but lay members who need direction and guidance on spiritual living in their everyday lives. Pastors are a local authority, limited in their authority to the congregation assigned to them.

- **Teacher** – Meaning "one who teaches." The work of a teacher is pretty self-explanatory: teachers teach things (Isaiah 30:20-21, James 3:13-14). In church, they teach spiritual things to whomever God calls them to work with (Deuteronomy 4:1-10, 2 Timothy 2:22, Titus 2:4-7). A teacher may work with children, youth, or adults, and they may work in the local church, in an institution designed to educate as pertains to church, or in the universal church. Like evangelists, they may have a universal scope of authority (beyond a local congregation), without formalized church authority (meaning they are not superior to universal or local authorities, but they operate a position parallel to such that relates to the growth and management of the church) (1 Corinthians 12:27-31).

WHY IS ORDINATION IMPORTANT?

Whereunto I am ordained a preacher, and an apostle,
(I speak the truth in Christ, and lie not;) a teacher of the Gentiles in faith and verity.
- I Timothy 2:7

Ordination is important because it is a confirmation of the work God is doing within that individual and the continuation of God's ministry within the church. Ordination serves as the anti-cessationalism: it is a lineage of proof, down to the modern day, that the Spirit is still alive and active; His gifts are alive and working in His people; and God is still calling people to active ministry by His Spirit, unto this very day. It presents the minister to the church, duly appointed by God and welcomed by leadership, to fulfill God's purpose in their life and ministry.

Ordination is also important because we need to have measures to assess the legal and proper order required by our governments in order to perform spiritual ceremonies. Anyone can proclaim that two people are married or that someone is baptized, but without the proper authorized paperwork, those ceremonies will not stand up from a legal perspective. Yes, we recognize that God is superior to the state and that spiritually whatever God says outweighs things in the natural, but at the same time, God has called us to be within legal parameters and to submit ourselves to governmental authorities (Romans 13:1). This means that our ceremonies should be recognized by the government as well as by God, and the way to ensure this happens is to do things decently and in order, holding proper credentials when we are in God's ministry.

WHO IS A CANDIDATE FOR ORDINATION?

There will I make the horn of David to bud: I have ordained a lamp for mine anointed.
- Psalm 132:17

Just because someone claims to be called to ministry does not mean they are called to receive the rite of ordination. Everyone is called to do something in this world; God has endowed everyone with gifts and has called us to use those gifts and make them fruitful. Just because someone is called to do something does not mean they should be ordained. In keeping with this, we can see the call to receive ordination clearly and the criteria that must exist for one to be ordained:

- Must be called to an office of the five-fold ministry: apostle, prophet, evangelist, pastor, or teacher or must be in a position that requires licensure or ordination (or both) for a specific ministerial task.

- Must be assured and knowing of their calling, with an understanding of what God is calling them to do and the purpose God has set forth for them. This doesn't mean they have to know every little detail of how God is going to work and purpose them in life, but it does mean they have to have a general understanding of the vision God is placing before them. As ministers, they should have proper vision and realize that ministry work involves purpose, dedication, and focus.

- Must have at least one year of educational training within the Word, the five-fold ministry, the applicable rites, rituals, and ordinances of ministry, and ministerial education. Seminary (at least three years) education is most desired, and in a world where we are getting farther and farther away from education and understanding within the church, seminary graduation or an experience equivalent should be required for ministers in training. This is not training in one's calling, but educational training which applies to making ministry functional and practical. All of us need to learn the logistics of ministry: the ins and outs of our calling according to the Word, the legal aspects of ministry, and teachings on the Spirit, the walk of the Lord, and training to see our calling alive and well within the Word. We cannot remove the educational aspect, which the Bible describes as "rightly dividing the Word of truth" (2 Timothy 2:15) from ministry. Saying that one is "called" or recognizing that someone can preach well is not enough to distinguish a true call to ministry.

- Must have a call acknowledged by leadership as valid and legitimate. This doesn't mean every leader in the world acknowledges it as valid, or that even every leader the individual has sat up under acknowledges the legitimacy of it. It does mean that the current leadership covering acknowledges the call of the individual as do others who have received of the Word through the individual and acknowledge its legitimacy.

- Must have the discernment to live the Christian life, despite the difficulties which may come from it; and is living that life, graced by the Holy Spirit. This doesn't mean a leader never makes mistakes, but it does mean they have reached an important place by which they strive for holiness and godliness in their life.

- Must walk in spiritual maturity. It's easy to be immature in the church today; the difficulty is standing as an adult amidst the flood of leaders who act like children. A person who can't stand mature in their faith is not ready to be ordained. Do we all have bad days, yes; this isn't what it is about. What it is about is having the ability to handle things within the church and that arise as an adult, rather than as a child. We must never forget that the Apostle Paul stated: *When I was a child, I spake as a child, I understood as a child, I thought as a child: but when I became a man, I put away childish things.* (1 Corinthians 13:11) This is a leader speaking an important word to us about Christian maturity, and here, I speak it to leaders: Put aside the childish if you want to be ordained!

- In keeping with the last point, maturity must be visibly displayed within the work of the candidate for ordination. This means that while none of us have it all together, a potential minister of God is handling their life as well as they reasonably can, managing their personal lives with decency and order, and managing their professional lives with decency and order. A candidate for ordination should carry themselves with dignity, avoiding the temptation to lash out at others or pout and behave childishly when they do not get their own way. They should support others who are moving up in ministry, even assisting at their ceremonies, supporting their own leader and assisting their leader in ministry, carrying themselves with honor and behaving properly (Hebrews 13:17).

IN DEFENSE OF WOMEN'S ORDINATION

The Lord gives the word [of power]; the women who bear and publish [the news] are a great host.
- Psalm 68:11 (AMPC)

This chapter about ordination would not be complete without answering the question about women's ordination. If there is one thing the church, as a whole, is most divided over, it is the issue of women. For thousands of years the church has engaged in debate after debate after debate about what to do with its women, as if they exist as set extras. Several thousand years later, despite better understanding of Biblical languages, culture, and history, we still see the debate rage, without an end in sight.

I could write an entire book on the defense of women's ordination, as one who has spent years in study of female apologetics. We could argue the issue left, right, and sideways, but I do not want to distract from the purpose of this writing. What I am going to do is make plain the issue and settle it simply.

First of all, yes, women are to be ordained. If women are called to ministry, they are called to be ordained. Do not make the mistake of thinking only men are called to be ordained. If we acknowledge the call of a woman to ministry, that means we acknowledge her steps are ordered of the Lord, and she needs to be duly appointed and ordained. Not ordaining a woman because she is a woman is indicative that a leader or group of leaders is somehow embarrassed or unsupportive of her call.

Second, the church herself is feminine. I am not sure why we conveniently forget this fact when it comes to leadership issues. It is illogical for the church to be feminine with an all-male leadership in place, turning away the women. If we are of the order of the church, put in place by the Lord, then we acknowledge the call of the church and her divine purpose in every woman who comes forth, called of the Lord, in the rite of ordination. If we have an issue with women, then we have issue with the church herself, because women are a type of the church, living and active, bringing forth life. To reject the woman in ministry is to reject the church herself.

Third, the defenses against women in ministry are of no contest in light of a true study of His Word, living and active, especially when we see the women of God in the Word as individuals who were real people, called of God, alive, breathing, and doing His work, duly ordered for His purpose. Stop trying to write away who they were and what they did; they are in there as a perpetual legacy for a purpose, a job, and a time.

In keeping with this, the criteria for ordination is the same for men and women alike. They must experience the same educational training, display the same character and maturity, and order. The rules are the same, which means exceptions are not made – for male or female.

TYPES OF ORDINATION

And He gave…For the perfecting of the saints, for the work of the ministry, for the edifying of the body of Christ: Till we all come in the unity of the faith, and of the knowledge of the Son of God, unto a perfect man, unto the measure of the stature of the fulness of Christ: That we henceforth be no more children, tossed to and fro, and carried about with every wind of doctrine, by the sleight of men, and cunning craftiness, whereby they lie in wait to deceive; But speaking the truth in love, may grow up into Him in all things, which is the Head, even Christ: From whom the whole body fitly joined together and compacted by that which every joint supplieth, according to the effectual working in the measure of every part, maketh increase of the body unto the edifying of itself in love.
- Ephesians 4:11,12-16

There are different forms of ordination, according to one's calling within the five-fold ministry.

- **Affirmation** – Apostles are affirmed. As the apostle is directly called by God and sent forth, an apostolic is an affirmation of that chosen anointing.

- **Mantling** – Prophets are mantled, signified by an actual ceremony in which the mantle is placed upon the prophet in connection with their call.

- **Commission** – Evangelists are commissioned to proclaim the Gospel, bearing Christ and the Word of Christ.

- **Installment** – Pastors are installed in their position as local leaders of the house of God. Their installment is in contrast to the apostolic, prophetic, and evangelistic in that they are purposed for a local congregation rather than itinerant work.

- **Appointment** – Teachers are appointed to instruct in the Word of God and with God's revelation on His Word.

VARIATIONS IN THE ORDINATION CEREMONIES

Beginning from the baptism of John, unto that same day that He was taken up from us, must one be ordained to be a witness with us of His resurrection.
- Acts 1:22

Different ordinations take on different levels and forms of formality. Some ordination ceremonies are very elaborate, while others are more simple. The level of formality within an ordination depends on the minister performing the ceremony and the understanding of ordination within that ministry setting. All forms of ordination require the laying on of hands and the issuance of ordination credentials in the form of paper licensure and certification. Beyond this, the variations in ordination take the following forms:

- A basic minister's ordination (non-specific to an office) usually requires the individual to preach their first public sermon.

- An affirmation requires a public acknowledgement of that individual's call to be an apostle.

- A mantling requires a prophet to have a prayer shawl (can be modern, specific to the ministry call, or traditional) and the ordaining leader to place the mantle on their own shoulders, speak words of ministerial relevance over the one being ordained, and then take the mantle off their shoulders and place it around the prophet being ordained.

- A commissioning requires an evangelist to be charged to go forth with the Gospel and an opportunity for the individual to expound upon a Biblical passage (such as Acts 8 or Isaiah 53) in public, before the assembly.

- An installment requires the ordination to be done in the church where the pastor will serve (at least at current term) and that they will commit to the duties and responsibilities of the pastoral office, serving as a spiritual shepherd therein.

- An appointment is acknowledged as a teacher teaches their first public lesson or class and is then confirmed to be serving in the work of the teacher.

WHAT IS NEEDED FOR ORDINATION?

For every high priest taken from among men is ordained for men in things pertaining to God, that he may offer both gifts and sacrifices for sins: Who can have compassion on the ignorant, and on them that are out of the way; for that He Himself also is compassed with infirmity.
- Hebrews 5:1-2

Ordination is a legal process as well as a spiritual one. What makes an ordination legal – and legally authorizes a minister to act in the office of such – is the minister's license given during the ordination process. Ministers should receive two certifications: a minister's license and a certificate of ordination. One, a license, is as a minister; the other is specific ordination to the office by which one is called. Both certificates require a ministerial seal by the minister performing the ordination (it must be the seal of the ministry performing the ordination, and not receiving it), the signature of the minister performing the ordination, either a board member or assistant to the service, and the appropriate date. The minister's license should specifically list what a minister is allowed to do (baptisms, communion, weddings, funerals, and in the case of apostles and prophets, ordinations) and should state that the individual is duly called to the work of ministry. The certificate of ordination should state the office the individual is called to. Both should contain the full information about the ordaining ministry, including the name of the ministry and the address.

For all ordinations, there needs to be a ceremony of the laying on of hands with both commissioning and prayer for the individual to go forth in the office to which they are called. This may be a private or a public ceremony, but it is generally understood that ordinations are public ceremonies. Apostles are affirmed to their office; prophets receive a mantling; evangelists receive a commission; a pastor receives an installment; and a teacher receives an appointment.

Aside from these elements, the rest of the ordination service is flexible. Most are done as a traditional service, with praise and worship, prayer, the Word, and preaching. Ordination services are also a special time to include specific elements to the minister who is being ordained, such as special music, dance, pictures, words, readings, or other elements that are unique and special to the ministry God has placed within that individual.

ORDER IN ORDINATION

But as God hath distributed to every man, as the Lord hath called every one,
so let him walk. And so ordain I in all churches.
- I Corinthians 7:17

As ordinations are an ordering of God's work, ordinations must be done within God's order. The only two offices we see performing ordinations within the Bible are apostles and prophets. Evangelists, pastors, and teachers can be ordained and can assist with ordinations, but are not offices that perform ordinations or ordain other leaders. The reason for this is simple: the apostolic and prophetic offices are the foundation of the church, the two offices by which all other leadership comes forth (Ephesians 2:20). The apostolic and prophetic are offices of order, each in their own way, and each with their own power. As they are specifically called as offices of order, it is most fitting that they are the offices of ordination.

ORDINATION FORMULA

For every high priest is ordained to offer gifts and sacrifices:
wherefore it is of necessity that this man have somewhat also to offer.
- Hebrews 8:3

The Bible does not give us specific words or mandates that must be spoken over someone during an ordination. The Bible indicates we must do the laying on of hands, and in the instance of a prophet, they are also duly mantled for their office prior to the laying on of hands. When the laying on of hands is done for ordination, the purpose is for the reception of the Holy Spirit for ministry, with the prayer and commissioning to go forth in ministry in Jesus' Name. The specific words used can be spoken by the Spirit at the time, given and deposited in the life of the individual, at the time of ordination.

MINISTER PRESENTATION

All these which were chosen to be porters in the gates were two hundred and twelve.
These were reckoned by their genealogy in their villages,
whom David and Samuel the seer did ordain in their set office.
- 1 Chronicles 9:22

Ordination is both serious and joyous. This means all ministers who participate in ordination need to both look and present the part of their ministries and ordered callings. Even though ordinations are often done in a church or with a church service, ordinations aren't just another church service. In recognizing God's work within the individual, the ordering of the church and ministry, and the continuation of the church until Jesus comes back, this is an important service. Within it we find the past, with our cloud of witnesses, those leaders who paved the way for us to be where we are in the faith; our present, in what God is doing for us here and now; and our future, the future of the church, and those who shall hear our words and come unto the Lord, in turn, hearing His call, and preparing for their call in their time. Ordination is a meeting of past and present; heaven and earth; and Kingdom and individual, all in this one time and moment.

The minister of God should present themselves formally for ordination. This is true for the minister performing the ordination, any ministers assisting in the ordination, and the minister receiving the rite of ordination. Ordination is an occasion for robes or collars and appropriately colored shirts, prayer mantles or shawls, formal suits, and white suits or dresses for women, if they are not accustomed to wearing formal ministerial robes. All involved should wear proper dress shoes, be neatly groomed, clean, and appropriately purposed for the task at hand.

Many have questions about what color shirt to wear, and when if a shirt and collar is called for in a ceremonial situation. In years past, we saw our ministers wear suits or black shirts with a full or tab collar. Because interest has grown in creating designations between the offices, a color system has been put into place to identify offices through the color shirts they wear. The problem with the system is that it does vary depending on the ministry involved in the ordination. If you are in doubt about what color shirt to wear for an ordination (whether you are being ordained or attending the event), it is advisable to ask. Others are confused about what to wear when people use specific terms that are unfamiliar. In my book, *Ministry School Boot Camp: Training For Helps Ministry, Appointments, and Beyond* (Righteous Pen Publications, 2013), I provide the following guide on the specifics of both civic and ceremonial attire:

Civic attire is, in many ways, making a comeback in many ministry circles. Even though it may not be an attire required on a regular basis, it is important to know the basics of civic attire.

It should be noted that the specifics on civic attire may vary between denominations and, at time, even ministries. What is considered appropriate or standard among one group may be totally inappropriate in another. Here we give guidelines, but if there is an instance where specifics are in question, it is best to consult with someone who can provide the specific answers.

The standard of civic attire is the white collar worn by the minister. There are two options for the collar: either a tab collar, which fits inside the neck of the shirt, or a full collar, which is worn around the entirety of the neck. Some traditions forbid the full collar to be worn by an individual who is not ordained as a pastor, apostle, or appointed as an elder (in this instance, a tab collar is required). Others require the tab collar when one is a licensed minister, but not an ordained minister.

There is then the shirt itself, which is worn with the white collar. The traditional and standard colors for a clergy shirt are white and black, which may be worn by any and all members of the clergy. In travel, black is the traditional color, although any color shirt with a collar may be worn as part of street wear.

- **Apostle** – Red (sometimes fuchsia or purple)
- **Prophet** – White (sometimes royal blue or navy blue)
- **Evangelist** – Gray
- **Pastor** – Royal blue or green
- **Teacher** – Light blue, green, or yellow
- **Bishop** – Fuchsia or purple
- **Elder** – Maroon
- **Minister** – Black

When dressed in civic attire, one must wear a black suit, one complete with jacket and pants or a skirt. Women should not wear pants when in civic attire, but a skirt of appropriate, below-the-knee length. Men should wear black socks and shoes, and women black pantyhose and formal dress shoes. Jewelry should be kept to a minimal, with the exception of a silver or gold cross, worn with a specific color cord (that should be specified by the ministry).

Ceremonial attire varies depending on the church or ministry you are dealing with. It also varies depending upon the event at hand. Ceremonial attire can be very simple or very elaborate. Below are some of the basics of ceremonial pieces and what they are.

- **Cassock Robe** – A basic preaching robe that buttons up the front and is worn like a long jacket. Cassock robes are worn for preaching or for more formal events by those who are not much for robes on a regular basis. They come in a variety of colors and styles.

- **Chasuble** – The outer garment worn in a formal setting that slips over the head and is free-fitting on both sides, without sleeves. They come in many colors and match the liturgical season or feast color of the day.

- **Alb** – The plain white garment worn as the base of all formal ceremonial attire in liturgical circles.

- **Cincture** – A rope band worn around the waist of an alb.

- **Stole** – A colorful and embroidered scarf that hangs around the neck and down the front of the body, usually fringed at the end. It is worn under the chasuble.

- **Prayer shawl/mantle** – A garment for prayer worn wrapped around the shoulders and back, meeting in the front of the body. A prayer shawl may represent a traditional Jewish appearance, with the fringes and Hebrew lettering, or may be knitted or modern, made to represent more of a modern interpretation of the garment.

- **Mitre** – The large hat worn by a bishop and, in some circles, an apostle.

- **Yarmulke** – The small pink or red skullcap worn by Jewish men and sometimes Messianic adherents.

- **Cope** – the outer-cape worn to match the liturgical cassock worn by a minister. Traditionally used for outdoor functions.

On a spiritual note, prior to ordination, all involved – both in leadership and reception – should engage in prayer, focus, and vision from the Lord for the event. When a sermon or message is delivered, it should be delivered by the minister performing the ordination. Bible verses and Scripture readings should attend to both the specific calling of the minister at hand and the office to which they are called. All leaders involved in the ceremony should share duties such as reading the Word, praying, expressing interest in the event, and talking to guests present. A welcoming spirit should be present, considering the different callings, spiritual understandings, and perspectives of those who may be invited to witness this event. Family, friends, members, and both saved and unsaved are often present at the ordination of a minister, which means the ceremony also stands as a witness of God's transforming and saving work within His people.

ORDINATION PREPARATION

Before I formed thee in the belly I knew thee; and before thou camest forth out of the womb I sanctified thee, and I ordained thee a prophet unto the nations.
- Jeremiah 1:5

It was said earlier that prior to ordination, a minister should engage in no less than six months to one year of ministry educational training. Traditional standards for ministry preparation were three years, in the form of seminary education. In Old Testament times, prophets were trained and set apart for their ministries through the school of the prophets. The school of the prophets was far more than just a six-week course or a few month-course devoted to rehashing different versions of a leader's teachings. Some schools of the prophets (1 Samuel 19:18-24, 2 Kings 2:1-18, 2 Kings 4:38-44) were thirty years or more. The school of the prophets evolved into seminary through the understanding of a "seminal" education, believing that seminary planted a necessary educational seed within a candidate to handle ministry. Because seminary was viewed as a preparation rather than a long-term connection or maintenance that one would receive through their denomination, seminary was set at the specific and spiritually significant length of three years. As an advocate of education, I still believe in the standard of seminary education; however, I also acknowledge that different circumstances and callings stipulate different needs and amounts of education. For example, someone who has been operating in ministry for a number of years without ordination does not need the same amount of preparation training as someone who is just starting out and learning the ins and outs of ministry purpose. Likewise, someone who seeks to do outreach ministry as a primary function of their office does not have the same preparatory needs as someone who is going to function in pulpit ministry. For this reason, we need to consider the individual's needs when they come to us in ministry. Apostolic University offers complete three-year seminary, recognizing the purposes of people in ministry are different, and God's training and purposing equates to different experiences and needs in individuals preparing for ordained ministerial work. As a result, we seek to include specified training for those who are in the five-fold along with general seminary studies.

If an individual is being trained by an organization for ordination or licensing, they need education in at least the following topics. Do not assume that someone has been attending a church for a long time:

- **Ministry:** What it is, what does it mean to be in it, and what is the essence of a minister's heart.

- **Spiritual education:** Instruction in matters such as the five-fold ministry, where their specific office fits within the five-fold, interactions with other members of the five-fold, the functions of the church, and the gifts and fruit of the Spirit.

- **Biblical education:** General Bible education, education on specific books of the Bible, contents, differences in Biblical books and teaching, hermeneutics, exegesis, context, history, and culture.

- **Leadership:** Specific studies in the Word as pertain to and about leaders, leadership maturity and conduct, and God's expectations of leaders within the five-fold ministry.

- **Office:** Call and duties as are found within the Word, and the specifics of the office as found in the Word.

- **Legal preparations:** 501(c)(3), state laws governing ministry, and any applicable ministry regulations.

- **Practical ministry:** Communication, public speaking, altar work, ability to communicate with others (such as foreign language instruction), discernment of behavior and reading interactions with others, and engaging others to participate in ministerial work.

- **Social Gospel ministry:** Training in at least one ministry that can apply to the betterment and witness of humanity, such as counseling, a specific work found in Matthew 25 (feeding program, clothing program, prison ministry, shut-in ministry, clean water program, etc.), men's or women's ministry, children or youth ministry, or some other project that interacts with people and betters the community.

Those preparing for ordination should show competency in these areas of education prior to ordination, either through testing, projects, or some other competency examination. It is also important to state that an ordaining minister should have some sort of relationship with the individual being ordained, the education they receive or are recommended to receive, and in seeing the requirements are completed in full. The process should not just be done by any leader, but by the individual's leader, and assisted by mentors and supporters. Ordination isn't just a spiritual commissioning and equipping, it is also a transfer; not in the sense that the ordaining minister is replaced, but in a sense that the grace which God has bestowed to one leader is the common unction of all leaders, and is given as a gift to the newly ordained, as well.

Prior to the ordination ceremony, the ordaining minister should meet with the ordination candidate to discuss the ceremony. Any special or unique touches to the service should be discussed and embraced, the ceremony planned, and the date selected.

CEREMONY

Ordination ceremonies generally follow the format of a regular service, with some special additions. Below is a general outline for an ordination service, which can be modified or added to as necessary.

- Prayer

- Praise & Worship

- Welcome, greetings, and opening words

- Opening prayer

- Reading of scripture/special reading selection

- Sermon/Preaching of the Word

- Public acknowledgement/examination/recitation by the minister being ordained (if required)

- Affirmation or mantling (if required)

- Ordination (Laying on of hands/Mantling)

- Special selection by the minister being ordained

- Communion

- Presentation of certificates

- Presentation of the ordained minister

- Prayer

- Song

- Dismissal

ORDINATION DOS AND DON'TS:

- DO uphold the relevance and importance of ordination, as it is part of God's order.
- DO recognize the evidence of God's continuation of ministry present in ordination.
- DO uphold criteria for ordination: Called to an office of the five-fold, assured in that calling, six months to one year of educational training, acknowledged call, discernment to live the Christian life, and walk in spiritual maturity.
- DO recognize the differences in the five-fold ministry and their differences in training and ordination.
- DO understand the different types of ordination: affirmation, mantling, commissioning, installment, and appointment.
- DO see that ordination is legal as well as spiritual.
- DO present the part of an ordaining minister or assisting minister, dressed appropriately and appropriately presenting one's self and one's ministry.
- DO observe God's order in ordination: ordinations are done by apostles and prophets.
- DO implement balanced and essential training for those in ministry.
- DO be a leader, knowing those you ordain.

- DON'T treat ordination as if it doesn't really matter.
- DON'T assume that everyone who requests ordination is qualified to be ordained.
- DON'T ignore essential education and information needed for ordination qualification.
- DON'T refuse to ordain women.
- DON'T treat every single ordination as if it's exactly the same.
- DON'T forsake God's order in ordination.

FEMALE DEACONESSES AND ELDERS

CHAPTER TWO

Appointments

And when they had ordained them elders in every church,
and had prayed with fasting, they commended them to the Lord,
on Whom they believed.
- Acts 14:23

WHAT ARE APPOINTMENTS?

This is a true saying, if a man desire the office of a bishop, he desireth a good work.
- 1 Timothy 3:1

Appointments are the works of ministry established to assist the five-fold (especially apostles and pastors) in purpose and function: namely, the works of bishop, elder, and deacon. These are not ministry callings, nor are they offices of ministry, but are ordered ministry works designed to assist the five-fold in function and operation.

Appointments are so-called because the individual is being appointed, for a period of time (it may be for a long period of time or a short period of time) to assist in the work of ministry. This is in contrast to a ministry calling, which is given by God and irrevocable (Romans 11:29). Those who work in appointments are a part of the helps ministry and are ordained to their function within the Kingdom. Their ordinations are not in the same sense as a ministry ordination, but as in their work of helps is ordered by the Lord and they need the endowment of the Holy Spirit by which to execute their work.

WHY DO WE NEED APPOINTMENTS?

Then the twelve called the multitude of the disciples unto them, and said,
It is not reason that we should leave the word of God, and serve tables.
Wherefore, brethren, look ye out among you seven men of honest report, full of the Holy Ghost and wisdom,
whom we may appoint over this business.
- Acts 6:2-3

The New Testament reveals to us that the five-fold ministry's main purpose (especially that of the apostle) is ministry work – not secular work (Acts 6:2-3). Modern ministry testifies to the grave difficulty five-fold ministers face when they must financially support families and the work of God. There is no end to the vast number of needs present within the Kingdom and no end to the ability to meet them. Appointments serve to help meet the needs of the Kingdom so the five-fold ministry can attend to ministry AND the Kingdom needs may be met, without over-extending ordained ministers.

The original "ministry of helps" is found in the appointments of bishop, elder, and deacon. In seeing appointments like this, they are essential to the proper function of the church. The catch is that bishops, elders, and deacons must function as they are Biblically ordered to do so, rather than creating ministries for them which represent a disordered purpose.

BISHOPS, DEACONS, AND ELDERS

And the apostles and elders came together for to consider of this matter.
- Acts 15:6

Sometimes we see bishops having more weight and control in the church than apostles. It's not uncommon to see deacons run the churches in some denominations, and elders are often thought akin to pastors. These roles are not the appointed, established appointments set forth in God's Word for bishops, deacons, and elders.

A bishop is an "overseer." This means that a bishop oversees something. A bishop's appointment is to oversee something established by a five-fold minister, to help when the minister cannot be present. They may be appointed to oversee a division of ministry, a church, a specific social or helps ministry, a region or district, or some other area of the ministry that needs direction and attention in a way the minister cannot give it and attend to the work of the ministry (Acts 1:20, Philippians 1:1, 1 Peter 2:25). It should also be noted that the term "bishop" is used, on occasion in the New Testament, to refer to the overseeing work of apostles in covering ministry. This further helps us define the purpose of a bishop, as can be seen in places such as 1 Peter 2:25. It clarifies that the ministry work of a bishop is to oversee something, monitor something, and establish an order with something.

A deacon is appointed to the ministry of helps. It is the deacon's job to see to it that the social needs of people within the church are met. Deacons assist in the distribution of helps as needed, assist in the financial aspects of ministry, and assist ministers of the five-fold in their ministering, duties, and purpose (Acts 6:2-8).

The term "elder" is used three ways in the Word. The first way is to indicate someone is of an older age (Luke 15:15, Romans 9:12, 1 Timothy 5:1-2). The second way is to indicate a superior in ministry, as in one who is of a higher office than another (Exodus 19:7, Joel 2:16, 1 Timothy 5:19). The third way is to refer to the "elders of the church," as in individuals who serve as overseers of sort, just over a local congregation (Acts 25:15, 1 Timothy 5:17, Titus 1:5). The elders of the church are appointed to assist in overseeing the needs of a congregation. In some instances, the term "elder" also applies to pastors in a specified sense (such as pastors over a ministry work within a ministry – a church's youth pastor, women's pastor, children's pastor, etc.), and pastors may, at times, serve in a functional role as elders over a church, especially if elders or other appointments are not present. For this reason, the criteria for elders is often used as the criteria to select a pastor, even though the Biblical criteria for elders and pastors is different.

CONFUSION IN THE ROLE AND WORK OF THE APPOINTMENTS

Then Peter, filled with the Holy Ghost, said unto them, Ye rulers of the people, and elders of Israel,
If we this day be examined of the good deed done to the impotent man, by what means he is made whole;
Be it known unto you all, and to all the people of Israel, that by the Name of Jesus Christ of Nazareth,

whom ye crucified, whom God raised from the dead, even by Him doth this man stand here before you whole.
- Acts 4:8-10

If you think a bishop is a superior office to an apostle, that apostles should be covered by bishops, that elders and pastors are the same thing, or that bishops are just another word for pastors, you came to these conclusions due to confusing teaching that attempts to merge the five-fold and the appointment ministries. The reason this happened is simple: when the post-apostolic leaders started to take over the church, they set up the system of priests, deacons, and bishops within their churches rather than the five-fold ministry and the appointments. The result is centuries of churches and denominations with all sorts of leadership concoctions within their ranks, but almost always, with bishops at the authoritative helm. This has given many the impression that the head of every ministry, church, and organization, there should be a bishop. Fast-forward to today, now that we are reintroducing the five-fold ministry to the church, people aren't sure where the five-fold always fits in when it comes to leadership structure in organizations. So it's not uncommon to hear many different notions, none of which are true, and all of which distort the work of the five-fold and the appointments.

Understanding the relevance in the appointment ministries shows just how important the work of helps is within the church. It doesn't diminish helps; it raises them up. It shows that all of us are important and all of us have equally important roles within the Kingdom. They may be different, but the Kingdom requires all of us, working together, doing the work that we are best suited to do, for the greater glory of God.

WHO IS A CANDIDATE FOR APPOINTMENT?

The elder unto the well beloved Gaius, whom I love in the truth.
- 3 John 1:1

The Bible lists extensive criteria for each appointment. The appointed criteria is essential because it proves the work of helps is just as important as five-fold ministry. If a minister can't trust the individual appointed to help them, the ministry is not being helped. Appointments are about reputation and good character as much as they are about doing good things.

- **Bishops** – *This is a true saying, if a man desire the office of a bishop, he desireth a good work. A bishop then must be blameless, the husband of one wife, vigilant, sober, of good behaviour, given to hospitality, apt to teach; Not given to wine, no striker, not greedy of filthy lucre; but patient, not a brawler, not covetous; One that ruleth well his own house, having his children in subjection with all gravity; (For if a man know not how to rule his own house, how shall he take care of the church of God?) Not a novice, lest being lifted up with pride he fall into the condemnation of the devil. Moreover he must have a good report of them which are without; lest he fall into reproach and the snare of the devil.* (1 Timothy 3:1-7)

In other words: Bishops cannot be people who are difficult, polygamous, active drunks, of poor character, selfish, greedy, violent, abusive, or poor leaders within their households. It is also clarified that bishops cannot be new believers.

- **Deacons** - *Likewise must the deacons be grave, not doubletongued, not given to much wine, not greedy of filthy lucre; Holding the mystery of the faith in a pure conscience. And let these also first be proved; then let them use the office of a deacon, being found blameless. Even so must their wives be grave, not slanderers, sober, faithful in all things. Let the deacons be the husbands of one wife, ruling their children and their own houses well. For they that have used the office of a deacon well purchase to themselves a good degree, and great boldness in the faith which is in Christ Jesus.* (1 Timothy 3:8-13)

Wherefore, brethren, look ye out among you seven men of honest report, full of the Holy Ghost and wisdom, whom we may appoint over this business. But we will give ourselves continually to prayer, and to the ministry of the word. And the saying pleased the whole multitude: and they chose Stephen, a man full of faith and of the Holy Ghost, and Philip, and Prochorus, and Nicanor, and Timon, and Parmenas, and Nicolas a proselyte of Antioch. (Acts 6:3-5)

In other words: Deacons and deaconesses must be serious people, not given to gossip, drunkenness, slandering, or faithlessness. Once again, they may not be polygamous, and must attend well to their households. They are to be people of honest report, full of the Spirit and wisdom, and well qualified to oversee the work they are appointed to oversee.

- **Elders** – *The elders which are among you I exhort, who am also an elder, and a witness of the sufferings of Christ, and also a partaker of the glory that shall be revealed: Feed the flock of God which is among you, taking the oversight thereof, not by constraint, but willingly; not for filthy lucre, but of a ready mind; Neither as being lords over God's heritage, but being examples to the flock. And when the chief Shepherd shall appear, ye shall receive a crown of glory that fadeth not away. Likewise, ye younger, submit yourselves unto the elder. Yea, all of you be subject one to another, and be clothed with humility: for God resisteth the proud, and giveth grace to the humble.* (I Peter 5:1-5)

In other words: elders are commanded to spiritually feed the flock, overseeing it, not with a bad attitude or for money, but of sound mind, not with control, but by example. Younger elders are to submit to older elders, and everyone submit one to another.

WOMEN IN THE WORK OF THE APPOINTMENTS

I commend unto you Phebe our sister, which is a servant of the church which is at Cenchrea: That ye receive her in the Lord, as becometh saints, and that ye assist her in whatsoever business she hath need of you: for she hath been a succourer of many, and of myself also.
- Romans 16:1-2

Controversy remains about the appointment of women to the works of elder, bishop, and deacon. I believe the controversy exists because we don't understand the appointment works in the first place. Seeing the role of bishop, elder, and deacon as positions of power rather than servanthood makes it sound like a power play rather than loving ministerial work. If we make the appointments a dominant power play, then of course there will always be male-female competition in the dynamics of structure. The answer to eliminate that is to eliminate the competition therein.

If we use the Bible to foster competition between men and women, we are always going to find it. Many read the Bible's words about a bishop "being the husband of one wife" means it excludes single men and women from the bishopric. This, however, can be answered with careful examination of the Scriptures. There are numerous statements in the Bible that are delivered in what is known as neuter tense – or masculine tense, which is implied to include women. When the Bible speaks of "sons of God," nobody reads that to exclude women. Even though it is a gender-specific statement, we do not think it is impossible for women to become a part of the Kingdom of God.

We tend to selectively apply gender-specific wording as we see fit. The issue of the bishopric is one such example. With the bishopric, one is "overseeing" something – they are fulfilling an assigned duty within a ministerial capacity. Anyone who is responsible for something is "overseeing" it – and, thus, we recognize a woman's ability to oversee matters. This same logic applies to the bishopric, and to all helps ministries, in general. The language is not excluding women – it was, most likely addressing a marital issue present in that day and age, which we shall speak of momentarily.

The criteria for bishops and deacons' wives were almost the same as for the men, indicating the women held a certain equal status within the community.

The specific nature of this statement is not just about men and women – if we take it so literally, it also excludes singles from serving in the bishopric. The issue was not one of whether or not a bishop was female or not or whether a bishop was single – it was a question as to whether or not a man who was a bishop could be married to multiple women. The prohibition here is on polygamy, or being married to more than one woman at a time. This practice was common in Greek and occasionally in Roman culture. Women and single people taking multiple husbands was not an issue; thus, it was not addressed. The Apostle Paul was affirming the exclusivity of marriage between a man and a woman, not the exclusivity of the bishopric to only married men. If someone desires to serve in the bishopric and they are married, they must have only one spouse, at a time.

This means if one is divorced and remarried, they must be legally divorced before they can remarry; if one is widowed, they may also be remarried; if one is single, they may serve as a bishop; and if one is a woman, they may also serve, given they are not living a polyamorous lifestyle.

WHAT IS NEEDED FOR APPOINTMENT?

And round about the throne were four and twenty seats: and upon the seats I saw four and twenty elders sitting, clothed in white raiment; and they had on their heads crowns of gold.
- Revelation 4:4

Appointments do not require special ceremonial items; they require well-qualified individuals who are duly prepared to help in the way God has called them to do so: through service. An appointment should be done as part of a service, either inaugural or a regular service, to appoint the individual to their work. A certificate of appointment may be issued for the individual who receives their appointment, commemorating the date and establishing them to their ministry work. It differs in that it is not a minister's license and does not entitle the appointee to perform the ministerial duties (such as baptism, communion, weddings, funerals, and ordinations), but does acknowledge the capacity of their purpose. If ordination papers or minister's license are required due to the duties the minister shall perform, those can be provided, as well. If the appointment is for a specific duration, this is specified on the certificate, which is signed by the minister doing the appointment ceremony, and sealed by the ministry.

CORRECT APPOINTMENT FORM

For they that have used the office of a deacon well purchase to themselves a good degree, and great boldness in the faith which is in Christ Jesus.
- 1 Timothy 3:13

There is no specific ceremonial rite for appointments. The only specified element is that they must receive the laying on of hands by an ordained minister, the one who is appointing them to their work. If there is a special element the individual desires, such as a Scripture that pertains to the work, or a song, that should be included in the ceremony, as well.

WHO ORDERS APPOINTMENTS?

And as they went through the cities, they delivered them the decrees for to keep,
that were ordained of the apostles and elders which were at Jerusalem.
- Acts 16:4

In the Bible, we see appointments ordered by apostles. The apostles, working in conjunction with the rest of the five-fold, and walking in their ministry, establish the order of appointments based on the needs and helps of churches and ministries. According to the Word, the work of the elders is also relevant in the ordination of appointments (Acts 16:4)

APPOINTMENT FORMULA

And let these also first be proved; then let them use the office of a deacon, being found blameless.
- 1 Timothy 3:10

The Bible does not give us specific words or mandates that must be spoken over someone during an appointment ceremony. The Bible indicates we must do the laying on of hands. When the laying on of hands is done for an appointment, the purpose is for the reception of the Holy Spirit for that helps ministry work, with the prayer and commissioning to go forth in their appointment in Jesus' Name. The specific words used can be spoken by the Spirit at the time, given and deposited in the life of the individual, at the time of appointment.

MINISTER PRESENTATION

For a bishop must be blameless, as the steward of God; not selfwilled, not soon angry, not given to wine, no striker,
not given to filthy lucre; But a lover of hospitality, a lover of good men, sober, just, holy, temperate;
Holding fast the faithful word as he hath been taught, that he may be able by sound doctrine both to exhort
and to convince the gainsayers.
- Titus 1:7-9

Appointments are both serious and joyous. This means all ministers who participate in an appointment ceremony need to both look and present the part of their ministries and ordered callings. Appointments, being done as a ministry of helps, is a reminder of the call among the Body of Christ to be of service, assistance, and participate actively within the Kingdom of God. This is why it is so essential for appointments to be done as a part of Sunday or other service, that the entire Body of Christ may participate and be present.

The minister of God should present themselves formally for appointment. This is true for the minister performing the ceremony, any ministers who may assist, and the minister receiving the appointment. Appointment is an occasion for robes on the part of a presider, collars, prayer mantles or shawls, formal suits, and suits or dresses for women, if they are not accustom to wearing formal ministerial robes. All should wear proper shoes, be neatly groomed, clean, and appropriately purposed for the task at hand.

APPOINTMENT PREPARATION

The four and twenty elders fall down before him that sat on the throne, and worship him that liveth
for ever and ever, and cast their crowns before the throne, saying Thou art worthy, O Lord,
to receive glory and honour and power: for Thou hast created all things,
and for Thy pleasure they are and were created.
- Revelation 4:10-11

Prior to appointment, the individual being appointed should receive training for the work they are about to undertake. They should understand the role of their appointment, the duties it carries, the significance of the work, and the importance of it. The preparation involved in training should relate to the duties involved in the work of helps, and the duration of time they will be involved in the work.

We also cannot undermine the relevance of the personal criteria involved in appointments. Evaluation of the established criteria is essential, which means the appointing minister must have a relationship with the individual being appointed. They must be the apostle over the church, ministry, or other work, in question. For this, pastors and other leaders should too be involved and consulted.

CEREMONY

The appointment ceremony, done as part of another service, consists of the laying on of hands. The recipient should come forward at the appointed time, either before, at some point during (such as after the sermon) or after the service. The individual should be brought forward, a Scripture reading read, prayed and commissioned with the laying on of hands, presented their certificate, and then presented to the congregation. If a special song is to be played or a special reading done, that should be done as part of the ceremony as well.

APPOINTMENT DOS AND DON'TS:

- DO recognize the relevance of appointments.
- DO see, uphold, and exalt the true ministry of helps present in bishops, deacons, and elders.
- DO uphold the criteria laid out for bishop, deacon, and elder.
- DO understand the work of the appointments, rather than confusing them with offices or works.
- DO acknowledge the work of men and women alike who step up to do the work of the appointments.
- DO prepare those who are to step up and assume appointments.
- DO see that appointment ordination is legal as well as spiritual.
- DO present the part of an appointing minister, dressed appropriately and appropriately presenting one's self and one's ministry.

- DON'T distort the concept of appointments.
- DON'T ignore the roles of bishop, deacon, and elder.
- DON'T think ordination of appointments is irrelevant.
- DON'T ignore the relevance of training for bishops, deacons, and elders.
- DON'T forsake God's order in appointments.

A WEDDING IN GREECE

CHAPTER THREE

WEDDINGS

I will greatly rejoice in the LORD, my soul shall be joyful in my God;
for He hath clothed me with the garments of salvation,
He hath covered me with the robe of righteousness,
as a bridegroom decketh himself with ornaments,
and as a bride adorneth herself with her jewels.
- Isaiah 61:10

WHAT IS A WEDDING?

Gather the people, sanctify the congregation, assemble the elders, gather the children, and those that suck the breasts:
let the bridegroom go forth of his chamber, and the bride out of her closet.
- Joel 2:16

A wedding is a ceremonial occasion, either civil, religious, or both, joining a man and a woman together in what is commonly called "matrimony." While traditionally regarded in a secular sense as a business deal between husbands and future fathers-in-law, we see shades of spiritual promise within weddings all throughout history, down to the present day. Weddings can be simple or elaborate, but all have the basic unit involved of bringing a man and a woman together in the preparedness and hopes of a joint future in life.

WHY ARE WEDDINGS IMPORTANT?

And there came unto me one of the seven angels which had the seven vials full of the seven last plagues, and talked with me, saying, Come hither, I will shew thee the bride, the Lamb's wife.
- Revelation 21:9

Throughout history, wedding ceremonies were used as religious, political, and business alliances. They were a part of social standing, stature, and celebration. The wedding ceremony was the ceremonial tradition sealing the business deal in which a man acquired a wife through her father or male relative. Over time, weddings grew to have a religious or spiritual significance as well.

We learn in the Bible that the return of Christ marks a wedding feast between the church and Jesus Christ. The church, often spoken of in feminine form, is the female counterpart, the bride preparing for the marriage to the groom. This means that marriage, in and of itself, is both a type and a reality. Marriage is a type of the relationship between Christ and the church, God and His people. It is also a reality: a shared love, commitment, and covenant established between a man and a woman.

The Bible establishes marriage as a necessary institution this side of heaven. It offers benefits, joys, challenges, and legal rights for the couple and their families. The wedding celebration is a reminder of the Bible's establishment of human relationships, the relationship between husband and wife, and the relationship between Christ and the church. It also holds prophetic significance, as it is a foretelling of the meeting of Christ and His bride in the last days, and a reminder to God's people to remain faithful in covenant with Him.

We hear a lot about marriage today. Most of what we hear is either negative, speaking about its deterioration, divorce, or trying to find ways to fix relationships that are hopelessly broken. It is easy for a minister to adapt a chronically negative viewpoint to marriage, always talking about it in a negative or difficult context. In the midst of such negativity, we need a moment of optimism and hope. Weddings give us the opportunity to celebrate God-ordained, God-established relationships and remember the joy that awaits us as we approach the coming of our Lord and Savior, Jesus Christ.

HOW ARE WEDDINGS SYMBOLIC OF OUR RELATIONSHIP WITH GOD?

Husbands, love your wives, even as Christ also loved the church, and gave Himself for it;
That He might sanctify and cleanse it with the washing of water by the word, That He might present it to Himself
a glorious church, not having spot, or wrinkle, or any such thing; but that it should be holy and without blemish.
So ought men to love their wives as their own bodies. He that loveth his wife loveth himself.
For no man ever yet hated his own flesh; but nourisheth and cherisheth it, even as the Lord the church:
For we are members of His body, of His flesh, and of His bones. For this cause shall a man leave
his father and mother, and shall be joined unto his wife, and they two shall be one flesh.
This is a great mystery: but I speak concerning Christ and the church. Nevertheless let every one of you
in particular so love his wife even as himself; and the wife see that she reverence her husband.
- Ephesians 5:25-33

The church exists in covenant with God, which is illustrated throughout the Bible as a marriage relationship between God and His people. As was stated above, weddings are a type of the wedding to come when Jesus returns. This special symbolism reminds the participants of four very important spiritual principles that relate to our faith and our walk of faith:

- **Honor** – Are we honoring the Lord as we should? The majority of the church would agree honor is an issue in the church, but believe it is someone else's problem. Husbands and wives are called to honor and respect one another, just as the church is called to honor and respect Christ. Honor is an action, brought about in how we speak of the Lord, if we obey the Lord's commands to us, and our general interaction with Him in our everyday spiritual walk. Weddings remind us of our command to honor the Lord and that such honor is not grievous or burdensome – it is what we do because we love and respect the Lord.

- **Love** – We use the word "love" on a regular basis in our culture. We say we love everything from coffee to reality shows and then come into church and say we love Jesus. This casual disconnect from understanding true love means we do not know how to uphold true love in our lives. Love is a principle, something that guides our decisions and is shown in our actions. It is something we do that reflects in everything we are. True love is shown. As with all things spiritual, love needs to find a starting place in a tangible sense, manifesting somewhere that trains us for the ups and downs and the ease and difficulty that love sometimes brings with it. Loving others sounds easy until we try to do it, and as a result, we need an immediate situation where we are trained in love for one another as we learn to live together as one. Husbands and wives are called to love one another, and to display that love in their conduct. Love of the Lord is also a spiritual principle shown through action. Jesus summarized the call to love best: *If ye love me, keep my commandments.* (John 14:15) Do you say you love Jesus? If so, how are you showing it?

- **Faithfulness** – The concept of being faithful is often regarded as outdated. In a world that changes at the drop of a hat, remaining faithful to anything is unheard of. Even though infidelity rates are high, God still calls those marriage partners whom He has called together to remain faithful to one another throughout their marital relationship. This faithfulness is more than a sexual fidelity; it is also a call to support and encourage one another and remain the biggest advocate of the other that could ever exist this side of heaven. We too are called to be faithful in our spiritual walk, because God is faithful toward us. Whether God has given us a ministry call, commitment, assignment, job, or life, we are called to remain faithful to that, no matter what we go through, as we work out our salvation with fear and trembling (Philippians 2:12). As believers in Christ, we see through our commitment to God unto the end.

- **Holiness** – Marriage is a call to holiness for both man and woman who choose to enter into the married life. As each partner comes into the relationship with issues, hurts, and areas in need of healing, both are given the opportunity to strive toward greater holiness as the marriage provides love and healing. Marriage is an excellent reminder to the call of holiness, that holiness is not always easy, the pursuit of holiness, and the walk of holiness in our daily lives.

Weddings are also important because they celebrate the life and bond of human love. It's an awesome experience to stand and walk with couples into their marital experience. Marriage can be a wonderful thing when the relationship is God-ordained and can bring each person closer to their God-ordained purpose. It is an opportunity for the Body to come together in unity to uphold the dignity and beauty of what God creates in and between His people.

CANDIDATES FOR MARRIAGE

Let us be glad and rejoice, and give honour to Him: for the marriage of the Lamb is come, and His wife hath made herself ready. And to her was granted that she should be arrayed in fine linen, clean and white: for the fine linen is the righteousness of saints. And He saith unto me, Write, Blessed are they which are called unto the marriage supper of the Lamb. And He saith unto me, These are the true sayings of God.
- Revelation 19:7-9

Marriage customs have varied through the ages. In New Testament times, marriages were arranged by families, between virgin girls and older men. By modern standards, especially in the west, this arranged marital custom is archaic and no longer practiced. It is customary for men and women of marrying age to seek out one another and marry after a period of courting and engagement.

That having been said, a marriage candidate is:

- **Of legal age** – Christian churches of all sorts should consistently refuse to marry persons under the age of 18, even when parental consent is involved. State laws pertaining to statutory rape vary, and a church or minister endorsing the marriage of minors can find itself in a very difficult legal situation.

- **Consenting** – Marriages should not be forced or arranged in modern culture. We do not live in a day and age where a female should be forced to marry a male due to pregnancy if they do not desire to get married. Parents should not meddle in their children's relationships, forcing them to marry someone against their will. In order for a marriage to be valid, both male and female need to consent to the relationship and agree to the marriage.

- **Not married to anyone else** – Even though polygamy is getting a lot of press these days, polygamous marriage is incompatible with Christian belief, life, and understanding. For a Christian to enter into a marriage with another believer, both parties must be legally able to marry (i.e., either never married or legally divorced).

- **Mature** – Maturity does not necessarily come with age. Someone who wants to marry at 21 may be just as prepared to marry as someone who is 31 or older. Signs of maturity include:

  - Knows what they want and seek out of life.
  - A desire to do as the Lord has commanded them, and are willing to uphold that, whether married or not.
  - Has obtained adequate education to participate in participating in the provision for a household.
  - Has a proper understanding of marriage and a realistic idea of what married life will be like.
  - Has enough understanding of themselves to recognize their flaws and imperfections.
  - Knows the flaws and imperfections of their potential husband or wife.
  - A good sense of responsibility and of the requirements of being an adult.

- **Stable in belief** – Getting married to try and work out issues with God is a good way to wind up away from God or in a very difficult spot spiritually. Marriage can enhance our faith in God when we are stable in Him.

- **Willing to follow wedding preparation procedure** – If someone is bucking against wedding regulations, the odds are good they aren't ready for formal marriage. One of the surest signs of a readiness for marriage is the willingness to follow the proper authorized procedure for wedding preparation.

WEDDING PREPARATION PROCEDURE

Let him kiss me with the kisses of his mouth: for thy love is better than wine.
Because of the savour of thy good ointments thy name is as ointment poured forth,
therefore do the virgins love thee. Draw me, we will run after thee: the king hath brought me into his chambers:
we will be glad and rejoice in thee, we will remember thy love more than wine: the upright love thee.
- Song of Solomon 1:2-4

Most churches have a preparation procedure in place for couples who desire to be married. There are a few guidelines to keep in mind for wedding preparations:

- **The needs of couples will be different and need to be assessed for preparation purposes** – An 18-year-old couple will have radically different preparation needs than a 30-something couple on a second marriage or a couple in their 60s on a second marriage due to a spouse's death. The preparations for marriage should not be a continuous textbook case, but something assessed based on the age, situation, and circumstance of the people present. Their maturity levels, marital and life experiences, and approach to marriage should all be considered when working out a preparation plan for marriage. Some couples don't require marital counselling, while others may need a few months to a year's worth of preparation before they display the readiness to get married.

- **Don't rely on the fact that people WANT to get married as a sign that they are READY to get married** – In the long-run, ministers cannot stop people from getting married, nor do we have the right to prevent them from getting married. What they can do, however, is do as much as possible to prepare them for marriage prior to their ceremony.

- **Don't over-do counseling** – Many ministers think the surest way to prevent divorce is to put a couple through rigorous, marital hell preparation training. The truth about any type of preparation for marriage is that it still isn't the real deal, and divorce is not something most couples are anticipating. A counselor can provide as much wisdom as they'd like pertaining to divorce prevention, but couples preparing for marriage aren't in divorce mode and won't give much credibility to it at this stage of the game. Pre-marital counseling should seek to establish good foundations for a marriage between couples – not avoid divorce. If martial counseling is seen as an equipping, there is no need to over-do counseling for months and months at a time.

- **Don't naturally assume people know about the basics of marriage because they want to get married** – There is a fairy-tale, magical element to marriage among many today. A starry-eyed bride is not thinking about the day when she and her future husband will fight over the dirty laundry on the floor, nor an excited groom anticipating financial struggles and fights with his future wife about money. People getting married may know a lot about marriage, or nothing at all. The basics of marriage should be outlined as a part of pre-marital counseling.

Good pre-marital counseling should focus on a few things:

- Helping a couple to learn good tools for marriage, including communication skills, marital partnership, healthy relationship dynamics, and dealing with relationship issues.

- Planning for family life, including financial and work arrangements, educational pursuits, children and the number of children a couple will have, if any at all, and the long-term goals and hopes of each partner in the relationship.

- Prompting the couple to discuss important marital issues together prior to the wedding, such as finances, sex and sexual habits and preferences, living arrangements, goals, visions, and shared duties and responsibilities.

- Spiritual issues, such as maintaining one's relationship with God, handling individual callings, prayer, personal growth and development, and the way spiritual matters will be addressed with children.

- Handling in-laws, family members, and friends.

- Changes to expect over the years (moves, changes in jobs, the death of close family and friends, illness, empty nest, etc.).

- Wedding arrangements and desires.

RECOMMEND TEXTS FOR PRE-MARITAL COUNSELING

Pre-marital counseling often becomes a seat for politics without a minister even realizing it. Too often, we, as ministers, get so caught up in concerns about marital statistics and about failing marriages that we spill such a nature over into our counseling approach. Marital counseling can become more of a session into marital failures than providing tools to make marriage a success, and it can happen without us being aware of it.

I have written two books that have proven very useful for pre-marital counseling: Discovering Intimacy: *A Journey Through The Song of Solomon* (Righteous Pen Publications, 2015) and *The Wedding Workbook: Your Four-Month Guide To The Wedding Of Your Dreams* (Righteous Pen Publications, 2015). Used in combination with one another, these two books set up a foundation for discussion, spiritual preparation, and ways that a couple can know each other better as they prepare for marriage.

INTERFAITH MARRIAGE

And unto the married I command, yet not I, but the Lord, Let not the wife depart from her husband:
But and if she depart, let her remain unmarried or be reconciled to her husband: and let not the husband
put away his wife. But to the rest speak I, not the Lord: If any brother hath a wife that believeth not,
and she be pleased to dwell with him, let him not put her away. And the woman which hath an husband
that believeth not, and if he be pleased to dwell with her, let her not leave him.
- I Corinthians 7:10-13

An interfaith marriage is a marriage where the two marital partners come from different religious backgrounds. Even though some go to the extreme of interpreting "interfaith" to mean Christians of different denominations (and I don't question that there can be serious differences in denominations), the general, accepted understanding of an interfaith marriage is when both parties are from radically different faith understandings that fall under the heading of different religious beliefs. An example would be a Christian marrying a Muslim, or a Muslim marrying a Hindu, or a Jew marrying a pagan. Most Christians are aware of passages that are frequently interpreted as forbidding interfaith marriage (Deuteronomy 7:3, Nehemiah 13:27, Amos 3:3, Malachi 2:11, 2 Corinthians 6:14-18). I understand the reason why these passages are interpreted in this light, and some of those reasons are practical, and some of which are spiritual. I don't believe if we truly understand what the Scriptures teach about marriage, however, especially in reading I Corinthians 7:1-24, that the Bible outright forbids interfaith marriage. I believe that, with New Testament understanding, it displays many reasons why it may be inadvisable and complicated, but that is different from saying someone will lose their salvation for marrying a non-believer. Unlike some religious texts, the Bible does recognize interfaith marriage happens, and it rises to the occasion to provide guidance therein. The Bible's perspective from a New Testament perspective is that interfaith marriage brings with it special conditions and complications. This means that, if people come to us who are of different faiths and desire to be married, we need to rise to the occasion and address the special needs that such a situation will have.

As marriage is a type of relationship between Christ and the church, it can pose an obvious problem when a believer marries a non-believer, as they won't understand the illustration. It is God's genuine desire that our marital relationships display His love, and teaching a non-believer about that can become complicated. Interfaith marriage can also cause immediate or long-term incompatibility with life, values, communication, priorities, and the way family life functions and grows over time. This doesn't mean such a marriage is impossible, but that such differences should be considered before a couple gets married.

When a couple of two different faiths comes forward, desiring to be married, the minister does not have the right to interfere in their own personal choices. If there is anything the Bible instructs us about, it is making it emphatically clear that people must make their own decisions on such personal matters. What leaders should do is promote and work the same type of intensive training they would with any other couple. Interfaith couples should be made aware of the challenges that lie ahead for them and how much more essential communication, discussion, and working together becomes when two people have many differences. An interfaith couple should see marriage as an invitation to discover truth together, in a new way, and as a family. Many of the issues that interfaith couples face are the same as any couple will face, but they must be addressed with more emphasis and introspection.

SITUATIONS INVOLVING DIVORCE AND REMARRIAGE

But if they cannot contain, let them marry: for it is better to marry than to burn.
- I Corinthians 7:9

Different denominations view matters of divorce and remarriage differently. For the sake of this book, I do not intend to expound too much on the ins and outs of divorce from a Biblical perspective, because I have found that how we interpret the Bible's teachings on divorce and remarriage stem from Biblical interpretation. I have taught extensively on the principles of divorce and remarriage in my book, *The Wedding Workbook: The Four-Month Guide To The Wedding Of Your Dreams* (Righteous Pen Publications, 2015). In it, I examine the culture behind the commands and explain much of what the Bible was trying to teach us about marriage, both from a cultural and spiritual perspective. I highly recommend reading it before trying to tell other people about their spiritual state after divorce, especially when it comes to remarriage.

That having been said, in this day and age, it is very likely that a couple will come to you, as a minister, for counseling, to preside over a wedding, or both where at least one (or both) partners will be divorced and seeking remarriage. Such circumstances don't require a special ceremony, but they do require special preparation. There are a few things that, as a minister, you should strive to assist with in such a situation. These include:

- Do the divorced individual(s) display a healthy attitude toward relationships?

- Do the divorced individual(s) display a healing in their lives, understanding how their earlier relationship(s) did not work out and what they can do to improve on healthy relationships now and in the future?

- Have the divorced individual(s) worked out existing hostilities with their former spouse to work out custody arrangements and child rearing (if applicable)?

- Has the divorce procedure been finalized, thus legally freeing the applicable individual(s) to marry again, freely?

- What special consideration has the upcoming couple given to the issues that relate from the former marriage, such as step-parenting and blending a family, child support, and spousal maintenance?

- Do both parties understand the relevance and importance that the divorced individual(s) with children play in the lives of those children and that no one should stand in the way of that relationship, including a new spouse?

- Do both individuals recognize the relevance in their relationship now, starting over again, learning from the past and committed to the future?

WEDDING PREPARATIONS

The king's daughter is all glorious within: her clothing is of wrought gold. She shall be brought unto the king in raiment of needlework: the virgins her companions that follow her shall be brought unto thee.
With gladness and rejoicing shall they be brought: they shall enter into the king's palace.
- Psalm 45:13-15

As part of pre-marital counseling, the minister must attend to the preparations and plans of the couple as pertains to their wedding. The basic marriage ceremony is simple: A Christian message, the recitation of vows, and the exchange of rings. All wedding ceremonies contain these three elements, and most also contain other elements special and unique to the couple.

Ministers must recognize what makes a couple legally married is the marriage license signed by both parties, the legally ordained minister, and the witnesses – not the ceremony itself. The ceremony itself is a profound experience of spiritual and practical meaning, displaying the hopes, dreams, and relationship a couple hopes to have. For this reason, weddings are more than just a message, vows, and rings. Couples should be encouraged to play songs or music of their choosing, be involved in Scripture readings or poems, write and recite their own vows, share pictures or videos, and involve family and friends in the day.

As part of pre-marital counseling wedding preparations, couples should provide the following information:

- What does the couple hope to convey most through their wedding?
- Best Man/Maid of Honor
- Parents of the Bride and Groom (or those involved in this process who they want to stand as representatives of such)
- Bridesmaids
- Groomsmen

- Ushers
- Ring bearer
- Flower girl
- Will there be special parts given to people in the wedding (step-parents, etc.) to celebrate their participation?
- Will the Bride be "given away?" If so, by who?
- Is the family using a wedding coordinator for the process? If so, who is the person who will be doing this? If not, what will the family be doing about matters of flowers, decoration, reception, and ceremony?
- Wedding budget
- Where will the wedding be held?
- Where will the reception be held?
- Date and time of wedding
- What "colors" will the wedding theme be?
- What special elements (music, Scriptures, dance, unity candles, poetry, readings, photos, videos, etc.) will the couple desire for the wedding?
- What unique touches would the couple like to have to make the ceremony their own?
- Will the couple be writing their own vows?
- Who will be involved in the clean-up process after the wedding?

WHO CAN PERFORM A MARRIAGE CEREMONY?

The voice of joy, and the voice of gladness, the voice of the bridegroom, and the voice of the bride, the voice of them that shall say, Praise the LORD of hosts: for the LORD is good; for His mercy endureth for ever: and of them that shall bring the sacrifice of praise into the house of the LORD. For I will cause to return the captivity of the land, as at the first, saith the LORD.
- Jeremiah 33:11

In the secular arena, a justice of the peace, magistrate, or judge are all legal avenues for marriage ceremonies. Within the church, a legally licensed and ordained minister is the legal option to officiate over a marriage ceremony. In order for Christian marriages to be legally recognized, a minister must be validly licensed and ordained, with both in good standing. In some states, the minister is required to file a copy of their license and/or ordination with the county or state. In others, as long as a minister is active within a church or ministry, they are only required to fill out the officiator's section after the couple has filled out their portion and file it with the county.

A couple should be informed and handle their part in obtaining a wedding license. Some states require fees, blood tests, or a holding period of so many days prior to a wedding ceremony. If they must appear in person to apply or file, they should do so prior to the wedding. A minister would then receive the applicable copy, fill out the needed parts, sign with witnesses, and file when the ceremony took place with the county registrar.

MINISTER PRESENTATION

Lift up thine eyes round about, and behold: all these gather themselves together, and come to thee.
As I live, saith the LORD, thou shalt surely clothe thee with them all, as with an ornament, and bind them on thee,
as a bride doeth.
- Isaiah 49:18

A minister is more than just an officiating figurehead in a wedding. The minister represents the divine connection in the couple's union, and stands as that representative before family and friends. It signifies the couple's desire to have God present in their marriage relationship and in their lives as individuals. A minister performing a wedding should not just crawl out of the woodwork for the wedding part and ignore the couple the remainder of the time. From counseling, to wedding planning, to the ceremony, to the reception, the minister should be present, standing, supporting, and encouraging. This also gives the minister a presence beyond the ceremony in the lives of a couple. Pre-marital counseling, officiating at the wedding, and attending the reception shows the couple that the minister cares and is willing to provide that representation if issues arise after the wedding, as well.

Weddings are a formal occasion for ministers. A minister should accord themselves with ministerial formalwear according to their custom or tradition: shirt and collar, robes and stoles or prayer shawls, dresses, or suits. Many ministers who preside over weddings seek to match the colors of the wedding in their robes or attire. The minister should be professionally presented, neat in appearance, put together, and organized. As is custom, women should avoid wearing white and red (robe colors are the exception to this rule, but should be adorned with a prayer shawl or stole), unless, for some reason, the couple requests it. Ministerial clothing should not be suggestive, inappropriate, or revealing, nor should it be obnoxious or loud. If a couple has a color theme, the minister should try to reflect the color theme in their attire. If the basic suit or robe is black, and the theme colors are purple and gold, accessorize it with one of the theme colors (a purple stole, a gold tie, a purple flower, etc.).

Ministers should be early to wedding preparations to assist as needed and answer questions or go over matters. If a wedding planner is involved, the minister should be involved in the design process as early as possible, especially if the wedding is taking place in the church or on church grounds – what is or is not allowed. For example, if a decoration is inappropriate or somehow dangerous to the church setting, that should be clarified. If alcohol is prohibited on church premises (as per the reception), that too should be noted. Any plans, prohibitions, etc. should be duly noted and worked out. Anything the church is planning to provide for the ceremony (tables, chairs, etc.), should also be noted. Fire codes and head count allowances should be provided to the minister ahead of time.

The minister should not forget their own spiritual preparations involved in a wedding. Wedding sermons and words should be tailored to the couple – not in a personal or intimate way – but should reflect the words God desires to give to that couple and the lessons God desires to teach us through their marriage. Before and after the wedding, the minister should be available to talk to guests, the family, and the bride and groom, and also be sociable and courteous at the wedding reception.

BEFORE THE SERVICE

He that hath the bride is the bridegroom: but the friend of the bridegroom, which standeth and heareth him, rejoiceth greatly because of the bridegroom's voice: this My joy therefore is fulfilled.
- John 3:29

Some people stand on a lot of tradition at weddings. They want the formal ceremony, family all seated accordingly, the bride given away by her father, the mother of the bride in blue, and a large ceremonial procession of bridesmaids, groomsmen, ushers, and the like. Other people don't look for so much tradition, seeking to have a wedding service that represents where they are in their relationship, what is important to them, and who they want to be as a couple. Some people want something formal, some simple, some basic, and several with something in between.

Because weddings are occasions which many stand on tradition (or at least part of tradition), I have included a form ceremony at the end of this chapter. The service can be modified and adjusted to the needs of the service, and can give a good overview of what people desire in a wedding ceremony. All the information presented here is to give a sense of order and establish structure within an event that, is in many ways, one of the most special days in the lives of a couple.

If music is to be played at a ceremony, the musicians should be present to play music at least thirty minutes prior to the ceremony, to set atmosphere and environment for the ceremony. General "setup" should be done within twenty-four hours before the ceremony (decorations and design), but not less than two hours prior to the event. Finishing touches (such as lighting candles) should be done twenty minutes prior to the event. Wedding photos should be completed no less than forty minutes prior to the event.

Everyone involved in the ceremony should be present for the ceremony at least two hours in advance for preparations and organizational purposes, in order to prevent chaos and unnecessary nervousness.

If a couple desires traditional seating, it is as follows:

- The bride's side sits on the left side of the altar, and the groom's side, on the right.

- The mothers always have the prime seating, first in the front row on each side. On the opposite side of the mothers are the fathers. In the case of a stepparent, the mother is seated with her new spouse or partner, or on her own. In that case, the father sits in the second row, with or without a new spouse or partner.

- Grandparents either sit on the opposite side of the father, or in the third row, if space does not allow them the room with the other family members.

- In the church, the last person to be seated is the mother of the bride, who is escorted by an usher.[1]

CEREMONY

Please note that the ceremony below is a standard traditional wedding ceremony. A couple does not have to follow this form of wedding protocol, nor should it be imposed upon them. This is a sample, basic format that can be altered, changed, or worked with – and is here to serve as a good guide for ministers. When traditions are changed, people should be informed, so they know what to do, and when.

The minister remains in the front of the church, at the altar, or at the place where the bride and groom will be married for the duration of the ceremony, as does the best man and groom. When prepared to start, the minister should notify the congregation that they may be seated at this time.

The processional[2]

- When the bride is ready, a wedding song begins, as selected by the couple. First in are younger attendants of the ceremony: flower girls, bridesmaids, and the ring bearer. They are typically followed by bridesmaids. Older bridesmaids and the maid or maids of honor follow. Most come in, in pairs, especially older members of the wedding party, with someone of the opposite sex. They sit in the front of the church, along with the family of the bride and groom. Once the entire wedding party has come in the church, the music changes to the bridal processional, and the bride enters. When the music changes, everyone should stand.

Introductory remarks

- **Minister:** We have come together to celebrate and witness the uniting in Christian love the wedding of (bride) _____ and (groom) _____. We know this union, relationship, and future is possible because of the Love of God, present to us today through His Son, Jesus Christ.

  1 John 4:10 tells us, *God is love.* So often we do not understand God's love. Many go through their lives never fully understanding this love God has for us, nor do we realize how love brings about change within us. The love of a couple reminds us of God's love, not just to one another, but to each one of us, as well.

  God shows us His love by bringing us together in love. (Groom) _____ has found and seen the love of God present in his bride, (bride) _____. (Bride) _____, has found and seen the love of God present in her groom, (Groom) _____. We know this ceremony signifies this love, and that His love is present within them both today and will be throughout their lives by God's grace and power.

  (Groom) _____ and (Bride) _____ are here to publicly declare that because God is love, they too can love one another, as love is from God. As God demonstrated His love through the life and sacrifice of His Son, Jesus Christ, our Lord, (Groom) _____ and (Bride) _____ seek to spend their lives demonstrating God's live by giving themselves in love, to one another and extending this love to those around them.

  Up to this point, we recognize the important role their families and communities have played in demonstrating love. Everyone present here today is here because of love, in love, and out of love to share in this day. We learn about love as we see it demonstrated throughout our lives. We honor and respect the love of those involved in their upbringing and development as man and woman, human beings, created in the image and likeness of God.

Giving away of bride

- **Minister:** Who then presents this woman for marriage to this man?

- **Father of the bride (or other representative):** "Her Mother (step-mother, family, etc.) and I do."

  (Groom should escort bride to altar steps or center, wherein the minister stands before them, facing the congregation.)

- **Minister:** If there is anyone among us who knows of any reason why this wedded union should not take place, he or she should speak now, or forever hold their peace.

  (Pause)

Prayer

- **Minister:** Lord God, we thank You for Your gift of love. We thank You for the opportunity to share in this day and celebrate the love you have placed between (Groom) _____ and (Bride) _____. We know that in this gift of marriage you have placed the promise of life, hope, love, and power within this couple. May they be strengthened by your love, and in learning how to show their love one to another. May we all be encouraged in their love, and in witnessing their love, hear Your call to be more active in our witness of love one to another. We pray this in Jesus' Name, Amen.

Sermon

Minister delivers sermon. All sit, including bride and groom.

Special selection of bride and groom

(Minister calls couple forward and introduces special section of bride and groom – musical selection, poetry reading, Scripture reading, etc. special to their service.)

Wedding vows

- **Minister to Bride and Groom:** _____ and _____, the vows of a wedding are sacred to a couple as promises made in earnest and kept through love. As you enter into the next phase of your lives together, your promise, your hope, and your future together lies in these words.

  If a couple is reciting their own vows, the minister will say: At this time, the couple would like to recite vows they have written themselves. (Groom starts, bride follows). If they did not write their own vows, proceed as follows below.

- **Minister to Groom:** _____, do you take _____, to be your lawfully wedded wife, to live together in the love of God; to love, honor, cherish, respect, and keep her all the days of your life, for richer, for poorer, in sickness and in health, and forsaking all others, until death do you part, for as long as you both shall live?

- **Groom:** "I do."

- **Minister to Bride:** _____ , will you have _____ to be your lawfully wedded husband, to live together in the love of God; to love, honor, cherish, respect, and keep her all the days of your life, for richer, for poorer, in sickness and in health, and forsaking all others, until death do you part, for as long as you both shall live?

- **Bride:** "I do."

(Minister has Groom take Bride by her right hand and repeat his vows to his bride. Then minister asks bride to repeat her vows to her husband.)

Ring vows

(Rings are presented)

- **Minister:** The wedding ring is a symbol of eternity. It has no beginning, and no end: much like love. Even though men and women meet and fall in love, with the beginning of their life together, love is something that has existed from the beginning with God. These rings represent the love of God and the eternal love designed to exist between a husband and wife. Here it stands as a reminder of the vows made between a couple, made of precious and valuable metal to stand as a reminder of the precious promises made between married couples.

  By exchanging these rings, a couple is signifying their promises, both to one another, and to the Lord.

- **Minister to Groom:** You may now place your ring on your Bride's finger.

- **Minister to Bride:** You may now place your ring on your Groom's finger.

Candle unity ceremony

- **Minister** – These two candles, one on the right, and one on the left, represent the lives of the couple, (Groom's) _____ and (Bride's) _____ to this day. We see their individuality, creativity, and gifts present from God flicker as they represent the Lord, the Light of the World. The middle candle represents their life together in God, one in His purpose. Today, they have come together, uniting their gifts, uniting their lives, uniting their creativity, together as one, represented as they light the candle in the middle from their individual lights. They are not losing themselves; they are not losing their identities in the Lord; but they are coming together by choice, in love, contributing what each has to create a united flame. No longer shall they be alone, but mutual in love and life; sharing in joys and sorrows, pains and blessings, in the eternal flow of the Holy Spirit of God. We know the Lord has said, *On this account, a man shall leave his father and mother and be joined to his wife and the two shall be one flesh*, and from the Word we consider what that means: *Two are better than one; because they have a good reward for their labour. For if they fall, the one will lift up his fellow: but woe to him that is alone when he falleth; for he hath not another to help him up. Again, if two lie together, then they have heat: but how can one be warm alone? And if one prevail against him, two shall withstand him; and a threefold cord is not quickly broken.* This light, lighting this center candle, represents that threefold cord: husband, wife, and God, that is not easily broken. May this light remind the couple to consider one another; rejoice with one another; support one another; and empower them in their lives as a threefold cord, always keeping the focus of the Lord as their true priority.

Sand ceremony

- **Minister** – Before us, we see two containers of sand, in two different colors. One represents the bride and all she is, all she has, and all she is to become; and one represents the groom and all he is, all he has, and all he is to become. When we put these two together, these two layered colors, these two beautiful reflections of the man and woman, we see a pattern develop, one that is indivisible and stands together in power and beauty. Now as they are poured together, they come together as one; bringing their uniqueness and purpose into one beautiful display, purposeful and ready to bring something beautiful forth to the world.

Communion

- **Minister:** As this couple has come together in unity, to become one, so we too remember the Lord's call to be one, His body, His people.

  (Communion ceremony follows)

Pronouncement

- **Minister:** For as much as (Groom) _____ and (Bride) _____ have consented in marriage, and have confirmed the same by standing before God and this congregation and reciting vows and exchanging rings; by the virtue, power, and authority committed unto me as a minister of the Church of Jesus Christ, and the state of _____; I now declare you husband and wife, according to the ordinance of God, in the Name of Jesus Christ, our Lord and Savior, Amen.

Embrace

- **Minister to Groom:** You may now kiss the bride.

Introduction

- **Minister:** Ladies and Gentlemen, may I present to you (Groom) _____ and (Bride) _____, husband and wife.

Closing prayer

The recessional[3]

- The couple exits first, followed by the flower girl and ring bearer, the bridesmaids and the best man, the parents of the bride, the parents of the groom, and the remaining guests row by row, from the front to the back, with the assistance of an usher.

WEDDING DOS AND DON'TS:

- DO teach on marriage, exemplify marriage, and show forth the spiritual lessons of marriage in teaching, rather than always trying to teach against divorce.
- DO meet with, work with, plan, and discuss with the couple beforehand.
- DO applicable pre-marital counseling, applying the plan to the unique circumstances present in that relationship.
- DO give the pre-marital couple activities and exercises to help prepare for marriage and marital communication.
- DO make yourself available for discussion with the pre-marital couple
- DO dress or coordinate to match the wedding theme.
- DO incorporate special elements desired by the couple into the wedding.
- DO work with the family and wedding coordinators.
- DO participate in the wedding, from the beginning to the reception.

- DON'T overdo pre-marital counseling, taxing and discouraging the couple.
- DON'T make the wedding ceremony all about you, the minister.
- DON'T wear exceedingly bright or obnoxious colors to a wedding.
- DON'T refrain from involvement in the process, hoping everyone else will take care of things.
- DON'T treat the ceremony as a legalistic, rigid experience.

A FUNERAL

CHAPTER FOUR

FUNERALS/HOME-GOING SERVICES

For I know that Thou wilt bring me to death,
and to the house appointed for all living.
- Job 30:23

WHAT IS A FUNERAL/HOME-GOING SERVICE?

Yea, though I walk through the valley of the shadow of death, I will fear no evil: for Thou art with me;
Thy rod and Thy staff they comfort me.
- Psalm 23:4

A funeral is the rite of memorial and burial for the dead. Within the funeral rite itself, there are many variances, which include a wake, the funeral service, and the burial. In addition, or replacement to these elements, there may also be a memorial service, cremation, or scattering of ashes. In the specific case of a home-going service, it is the funeral service and those same elements specifically done for a believer in Christ.

THE IMPORTANCE OF FUNERALS AND HOME-GOING

A good name is better than precious ointment; and the day of death than the day of one's birth.
- Ecclesiastes 7:1

Every culture and religion worldwide observes funeral and burial customs. The funeral rite is a final declaration, celebrating the life of the deceased, acknowledging their accomplishments, mourning their loss, and celebrating the individual's presence no longer in the body, but with the Lord in heaven.

The funeral process used to be a family and community event, in contrast with funeral process today, usually done through a funeral home or other systematic location. In days gone by, the body of the deceased was lain out for calling hours right within their home or their birth home, with family and friends coming forth to pay respects. This was followed by the funeral in the home and burial immediately after. The process had a more intimate feel to it, not so much systematic, but more intimacy with the life and relevance of the individual of the deceased. The older process had more connection with that person's life and what was most important to them.

Death used to be seen as going "full circle." Today people view death far differently than they did in earlier times. With so much fought against death at all costs, death sometimes comes as an unpleasant shock and reality, totally disconnecting the individual from their lives and loved ones. Because of this shift in understanding, death is often a complicated time in the lives of family, friends, and loved ones who are left behind.

It is inevitable for a leader to encounter the loss of a congregation member, friend, or ministry subordinate. At some point in a ministry, a leader will be faced with standing in the gap to perform a home going service and stand in support of the family, friends, and congregation that have lost a special and relevant person in their lives.

Leaders need to prepare themselves for the times in which they must take the role as leaders for funerals and home-going events. It is a delicate time in the lives of many, and this can lead to uncomfortable, if not awkward, circumstances that are not always readily remedied. It takes a special grace and training to be a good leader in a time of loss, inspiring hope and truth.

IF CHRISTIANS ARE ABOUT LIFE, SHOULD WE EVEN ACKNOWLEDGE DEATH?

So when this corruptible shall have put on incorruption, and this mortal shall have put on immortality, then shall be brought to pass the saying that is written, Death is swallowed up in victory.

O death, where is thy sting? O grave, where is thy victory?
- 1 Corinthians 15:54-55

Throughout the Bible, from Genesis to Revelation, we see a respect and reverence surrounding funeral customs. It was customary for individuals to prepare the body of the deceased, hold funeral and burial, and honor a customary period of mourning. Upon first glance, it seems like much of funeral custom centers around the deceased and the body of the deceased. On closer inspection, we can see something else entirely: funerals are also about the living. The loss of a loved one or friend can be a pivotal time in someone's life. Throughout the Bible, we see the following present in death:

- **Acknowledgement of the cycle of life** – As long as the earth remains in its present state until Jesus comes back, there will be birth and death, gain and loss, and getting and giving. God's work is cyclical rather than linear: prophecy moves in cycles, seasons move in cycles, and the spiritual realm operates in cycles. Death reminds us that life moves in cycles. In the end, we come to a place not far from where we start. Where God takes us on the journey in-between is exciting, powerful, and lively. We must celebrate and cherish what we have, what God has given us, and make the most of every day we have with Him.

- **Final things and new beginnings** – Death is the final aspect of one's life in this world. To many, it is only the end. If we believe in eternal life, death is not only an end; it's also a beginning. As long as we are in Christ, things in our lives both end and begin. In death, there is a new sphere of existence awaiting the believer. For those who remain, there are also opportunities to reassess priorities, situations, change, and examine themselves to begin again, begin new, or start over.

- **The promise of the resurrection and eternal life** – Death is not the end. If we believe in the resurrection, we believe in the life of the world to come. Eternal life is about right now as much as it is later. In the presence of physical death, we see spiritual life empowering all through the promise of the resurrection.

Funerals and events surrounding funerals bridge the gap between mourning and the call to move forward. In order to discover a new beginning, we must first close the end. Funerals provide a needed closure and period of grief and mourning necessary to allow God's people the transitioning period needed to move forward and advance the Kingdom in the presence of a great grief and loss.

FUNERAL PREPARATION FOR THE MINISTER

For this God is our God for ever and ever: He will be our guide even unto death.
- Psalm 48:14

Bible schools and minister training programs do not tend to train a minister in the necessary steps and preparations for funeral work. Most ministers 'wing it' when it comes to a very fragile and transitional time in people's lives.

Handling death and dying is not a simple task. Death and dying is as much about understanding the purpose and meaning in life as it is grief and loss. There are lots of ways to make mistakes, but also lots of ways to be successful and helpful. It is advised for ministers to take a death and dying course through a college or program (particularly one that uses the standard guidelines laid out by Elisabeth Kubler-Ross) to learn more about the stages of dying and be better able to identify circumstances leading up to death and profound loss. Such courses also help a leader employ counseling skills for an approaching death as well as an unexpected death.

Funerals and home going services often draw a larger audience than the immediate church crowds ministers may be comfortable with. A minister's funeral presence and message needs to be larger than the immediate church worlds we are all familiar with, and offer comfort to people who may be Christian, may not be Christian, may be something in-between, or may be dealing with confusion and questions about God even prior to this encounter with death. The call is to serve the role of a comforter, representing the work and ministry of the Holy Spirit in our lives. Ministers should be comfortable talking to others about death and answering questions about situations, processes, and Biblical beliefs surrounding the situation. It is to be expected that some difficult, hard-to-answer, and uncomfortable questions may arise. If you don't know an answer, offer to do some research.

On the practical level, a minister should be prepared to be present for the family in the wake of difficult decisions surrounding death and to stand as a comfort in times of grief, loss, and difficulty. They should also be ready and level-headed to stand objective when end-of-life issues arise. This means being present from diagnosis to wake and funeral, if possible. Ministers should have a basic funeral/home going structure that can be easily modified and adjusted based upon need.

Prior to a wake and funeral/home going, the minister should meet with the family or friends of the deceased (whoever is planning the service). It is important the minister knows the following:

- The name of the deceased as is to be addressed during services
- The last wishes of the individual as pertains to the funeral, if any
- The family/friends' vision of the event, including mementos, pictures, slideshows, music, and tributes
- Desired atmosphere for the event
- Funeral home involved in the process
- Open or closed casket or cremation
- Eulogies
- Pallbearers
- Assistant ministers
- Whether or not to hold communion as part of the service
- Any other feedback from the family about the event
- Day and time for event (not on a Sunday or during another service time)

WHERE ARE FUNERALS HELD?

Destruction and death say, We have heard the fame thereof with our ears.

When a minister has a relationship with the deceased or the family/friends of the deceased, the process of the funeral/home-going is often quite a bit simpler. A wake (calling hours) and home-going service are typically done in the church where the individual, family, or close associates attend. When a minister is called in for a funeral by someone who is not a member of a church or ministry, the wake and funeral are typically done in a funeral home.

When a funeral home is used for a funeral event, the policies of the home should be acknowledged and observed. Requirements may vary, as may the audience. When a funeral/home going service is done in a church, the atmosphere has more of a spiritual tone, and fewer restrictions. Ministers should accommodate the message and tone of the service to the necessary atmosphere.

Burial services are always held at a cemetery or burial site, while the scattering of ashes or memorial service may be done in any number of locations.

PREPARING THE BODY

Health laws stipulate the deceased body be prepared for burial or cremation within a certain period of time after the individual has died. In western culture, the preparation of the body is done by a funeral home. When a body is prepared for burial, it is embalmed to help slow down decay and help prevent the spread of contamination. It is also washed, dressed, and groomed for burial. Items of religious or personal importance may be included in the coffin and it is not uncommon for people to bring pictures or other sentimental items to place in the coffin during a wake or funeral.

When a body is cremated, it is burned until the remains are no more than ashes. The body is placed in a container specifically designed for cremation and then burned at exceedingly high temperatures. The ash remains are not considered a health risk and can be scattered, stored, or presented somewhere without fear of contamination.

THE WAKE

And Moses was an hundred and twenty years old when he died: his eye was not dim, nor his natural force abated. And the children of Israel wept for Moses in the plains of Moab thirty days: so the days of weeping and mourning for Moses were ended.
- Deuteronomy 34:7-8

The concept of a wake, or watching by the dead, is an ancient custom believed to be derived from the Jewish concept known as *shiva*. The wake is also known as "calling hours." While many ancient customs and concepts about a wake have followed protocol in their day and age, most modern wakes focus on support and respect to the family and friends of the deceased. Wakes are usually an expression of the person's life, what was important to them, and centers around his or her life and values. They are usually done in cooperation with the families and last wishes of the deceased.   Typically, the casket lies in state during the wake, usually opened, but sometimes closed. When a person is to be cremated, the body may lie in state during the wake, the ashes may be present, or the wake may just feature reminders of the individual's life, without the body present in any form.

In some unique situations, it is against the wishes of the family or deceased to hold a wake. These wishes should be upheld, for whatever the unique reason or circumstances.

THE FUNERAL OR HOME-GOING SERVICE

And, behold, there was a man named Joseph, a counsellor; and he was a good man, and a just:
(The same had not consented to the counsel and deed of them;) he was of Arimathaea, a city of the Jews:
who also himself waited for the Kingdom of God. This man went unto Pilate, and begged the body of Jesus.
And he took it down, and wrapped it in linen, and laid it in a sepulchre that was hewn in stone,
wherein never man before was laid. And that day was the preparation, and the Sabbath drew on.

And the women also, which came with Him from Galilee, followed after, and beheld the sepulchre, and how His body was laid.
- Luke 23:50-55

There isn't a right or wrong way to have a funeral service. The Bible does not give us specific words to speak at a funeral, at a burial site, at a memorial, at a wake, or at any other component of the funeral process. As a result, I am not going to give specific words or prayers to be said, as they are often very specific to circumstances and very relevant to the situations and state of the family at hand. The most important thing to do is accommodate any regulations and respect the wishes of the family. A secular funeral service may be shorter and may require a message delivered in a softer, less spiritual tone. A home-going service may resemble a normal service, complete with worship or inspirational music and a preaching message, with additional funeral components (the presence of the casket, prayers for the family, and requested additions to the event). The outline of how the service will go should be discussed with the family prior to the event.

Most funerals include music of some sort; prayers; reading of Scripture; a sermon or message from the minister; eulogies (words delivered about the individual's life from family or friends); additional prayers; and the carrying of the casket out of the church to transport it to the gravesite.

Funeral homes embrace three main components to funerals: Song, obituary or Scripture reading and prayer, Music, sermon or word from the minister, and a closing prayer. It is perfectly acceptable to embrace this format, or use something else as pertains to the wishes of the family. In using this format, my only recommendation is to use it as a guide, rather than a literal format for each funeral situation.

The only major thing considered "taboo" during a funeral is to take an offering. The traditional viewpoint of a minister's funeral work is that of a service provided by the church or ministry. Understanding funerals do cost money to the churches who provide this service, it is customary for the family of the deceased to make a donation or give a love offering to the minister prior to the funeral service. If a minister is travelling a long distance to perform a funeral service, it is also expected the family of the deceased cover those expenses. When a funeral is performed in a funeral home, the minister's expense is covered by the funeral home, rather than the family. On rare occasions, an offering may be taken to help the family cover funeral expenses (such as a poverty case or one where someone dies without insurance and the money to cover funeral costs). This money does not go to the minister, but to the family. Arrangements to take this collection should be made prior to the service.

BURIAL

> *So Moses the servant of the LORD died there in the land of Moab, according to the word of the LORD.*
> *And he buried him in a valley in the land of Moab, over against Bethpeor: but no man knoweth of his sepulchre*
> *unto this day.*
> *- Deuteronomy 34:5-6*

Burial is done at a gravesite or cemetery. Burials are often not large, public events, but may just be for family and close friends of the deceased. During burial, the grave is dug, the casket is lowered into the ground, and a flower is often thrown on the grave during the shoveling process. Prayers are said, Scripture is read, and songs or hymns may be sung grave-side. Once complete, those present depart.

CREMATION

> *In the sweat of thy face shalt thou eat bread, till thou return unto the ground; for out of it wast thou taken:*
> *for dust thou art, and unto dust shalt thou return.*
> *- Genesis 3:19*

Cremation is the process by which a dead body is burned. The only remains from cremation are bone fragments, pacemakers or other medicinal items, metal scraps (such as replacements or dental fillings), and gasses, which are released through ventilation systems. This is done in the west by a funeral home with a crematorium, and sometimes in the east, in an open air crematorium. The body is placed in a specific body container for cremation, and placed in an incinerator at extremely high temperatures. After the process is complete, the remaining bone fragments are ground, down to the state of "ashes" as we recognize from cremated remains.

Cremation may be done after a funeral service, before a service, in conjunction with a memorial service, or with no service performed at all. There are many reasons why people may choose cremation as an alternative to burial, which include finances (cremation is less expensive than burial), environmental (cremation is better for the environment), spiritual, or other personal reasons.

MEMORIAL SERVICES

And that these days should be remembered and kept throughout every generation, every family, every province, and every city; and that these days of Purim should not fail from among the Jews, nor the memorial of them perish from their seed.
- Esther 9:28

A memorial service is similar to a funeral or home going service, with a few notable exceptions. During a memorial service, the body of the deceased is not present in any form. People gather to pray, read Scripture, sing, pay tribute, or share memories of the deceased in an informal setting. Candles, used to symbolize memorial, are often lit or somehow a part of the service. Memorial services may be held immediately after someone dies in place of a funeral, or may be done on the memorial of someone's death, or done in circumstances in which a number of people die and a group of people desire to remember the deceased.

When a person is cremated, a memorial service may be held in conjunction with the scattering of ashes.

SCATTERING OF ASHES

Your remembrances are like unto ashes, your bodies to bodies of clay.
- Job 13:12

In cases of cremation, the ashes of the deceased are often scattered in the "scattering of ashes." This is typically done via a simple, informal ceremony done at a site of importance to the deceased. The nature of this ceremony varies based on the wishes of the deceased or the wishes of the family of the deceased. It may be done in a group setting, privately with family members and close friends, or done by a singular individual.

POST-BURIAL COUNSELING

So they sat down with him upon the ground seven days and seven nights, and none spake a word unto him:
for they saw that his grief was very great.
- Job 2:13

Some families and friends require more assistance after a loved one is buried and the funeral is over than you might imagine. The arrangement of preparations and attending to the needs at hand can sometimes delay the grieving process. This is especially true if an individual's death is very public or comes about by sudden or traumatic means. When someone first dies, there is an outpouring of support and memory for the loved one, and people come to comfort and assist the family due to the loss. After the funeral is over, people resume their normal lives and expect the grieving to do the same. It's often not this simple, nor so easy, for the grieving to do.

This where ministers need to step up and offer post-burial counseling and assistance to those they know who have experienced the death of a loved one. We need to show long-term support to the family, understanding their grieving process and standing with them as they go through different stages. Being there, listening, praying, showing compassion and encouragement, and supporting them as they make the difficult steps to move forward speaks volumes to the God we serve, Who we know is always with the living.

MINISTER PRESENTATION

And devout men carried Stephen to his burial, and made great lamentation over him.
- Acts 8:2

Funerals are a solemn occasion. Home going services are both solemn and joyful occasions. The living remember the dead, and they celebrate the passing of their loved one onto glory. As a result, funerals are considered a formal occasion. Ministers should dress formally according to their custom. In some groups, this involves a collar and shirt; in others, a robe; or still, in others, a dark-colored suit for men or a dark-colored suit or dress for women.

Ministers should read the Word, deliver the message, officiate at the service, and be involved in burial or scattering of ashes, as the family desires. Ministers should be involved prior to the funeral, greeting people at the funeral, and offering words of truth and comfort. The role of minister, representing comfort and truth, means the minister must be real-time, real person, accessible and easy to talk to. Ministers must be apt to listen, apt to support, and stand strong in the time of difficulty.

CEREMONY

As was stated above, funeral and home-going ceremony is very dependent upon the custom of a group and the wishes of the deceased and their family. The traditional elements of wake, funeral or home-going, and burial or scattering of ashes are followed in some semblance, based on the situation at hand. Little is available in a written outline for ministers in performing funerals. Here are some key things to keep in mind when officiating for a funeral, home-going, memorial service, or scattering of ashes:

- Keep in mind the wishes of the family, and uphold those at all times.

- Scriptures should reflect life, comfort, and eternity, as applicable.

- When reciting prayers for a group, stick to prayers that all can recite, such as the Lord's Prayer, or provide hand-outs with Scripture passages, prayers, or poems for all to recite.

- Do not forget about memorial cards (if not provided by a funeral home),

A basic guide for the service is:

- Hymn or song

- Opening prayer

- Obituary reading/words about the deceased

- Scripture reading

- Music

- Sermon or word from the minister

- Communion

- Eulogies

- Closing prayer

- Hymn or song

FUNERAL/HOME-GOING DOS AND DON'TS:

- DO stand as a comforting presence in a situation of loss and grief.
- DO make yourself available to the family, friends, and community in the presence of their loss.
- DO prepare for funerals/home-goings by meeting with the family, going over their applicable lists of funeral information, and the wishes of the deceased.
- DO respect the wishes of the family and the deceased.
- DO make it a point to know about the deceased and their family if you are unfamiliar with them.
- DO respect and honor regulations in conjunction with the funeral home, as applicable.
- DO participate in the process, from start to finish: wake, funeral/home-going, burial; wake, funeral/home-going or memorial

service, cremation, scattering of ashes; or any combination of circumstances that may arise.

- DO present well, dressing appropriately, and carrying yourself appropriately.
- DO encourage and support post-burial counseling.

- DON'T use a funeral as an opportunity to be judgmental, punitive, or critical.
- DON'T forge ahead with funeral or home-going plans without the family's approval.
- DON'T bully family members into a certain set of personal beliefs as pertain to end of life matters.
- DON'T ignore family members and friends who may not be members of the same church or local community.
- DON'T "wing it" when it comes to funerals/home-going services and memorials.

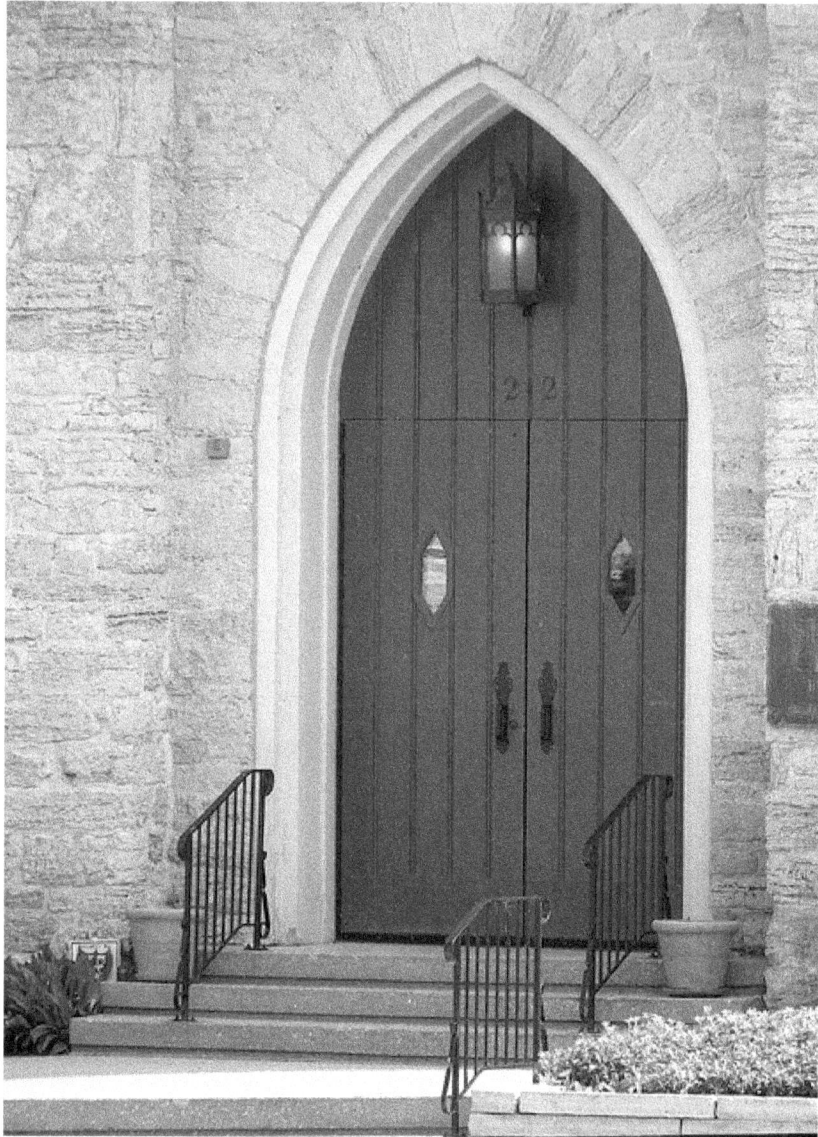

DOOR AND STEPS TO A CHURCH

CHAPTER FIVE

GRADUATION SERVICES AND SACRED ASSEMBLIES

But ye are a chosen generation, a royal priesthood, an holy nation,
a peculiar people; that ye should shew forth the praises of Him
Who hath called you out of darkness into His marvelous light;
which in time past were not a people, but are now the people of God:
which had not obtained mercy, but now have obtained mercy.
- I Peter 2:9-10

WHAT IS A GRADUATION SERVICE?

His sons used to go and feast in the house of each on his day (birthday) in turn,
and they invited their three sisters to eat and drink with them.
- Job 1:4 (AMPC)

I am using the term "graduation service" to refer to any service within Christianity today that celebrates the elevation or advancement of an individual in some way. It doesn't literally mean a "graduation" like a graduation ceremony from high school or college (although such an occasion can certainly be celebrated with a special service like these in church), but acknowledges that an individual is passing from one thing to another. Examples of graduation services include birthday services, a service where a minister is preaching for the first time, the first service in a new church or new building, a building dedication, pastoral anniversary, a graduation service celebrating the completion of a leadership program or a new believer's class, or a "watchnight" service, which is typically celebrated to pass from one year into the new year at midnight. There are probably other examples of graduation services that might be unique to a church or a locality that are not listed here, but can very much apply to the form and specialty presented here. The general rule for a graduation ceremony is it represents something unique to an immediate church or ministry rather than crossing boundaries and incorporating multiple churches within an event (although that is certainly possible with certain services).

WHAT IS A SACRED ASSEMBLY?

Sanctify ye a fast, call a solemn assembly; gather the elders and all the inhabitants of the land to the house of the LORD, your God, and cry out to the LORD.
- Joel 1:14

A sacred assembly is a formal occasion or gathering among an organization (typically beyond a local church) that gathers for worship, fellowship, and to handle ministry business, such as governance issues or the administration of rites among its leadership. An example of a sacred assembly would be what is commonly called convocation or annual assembly, which requires all members of an organization to be present to handle the different spiritual and practical business that must be properly handled. National, regional, or international conferences might also fall under this heading. Some organizations might also consider holiday observances, such as Old Testament feasts or New Testament observances (i.e., Resurrection, Pentecost), or more modern holidays, such as Christmas or Thanksgiving, to be under the heading of "sacred assemblies." A sacred assembly exists to display the unity, the need to handle organizational business, and to show that the church is greater than the local church by recognizing the church beyond a local church's borders.

Sacred assemblies in the Old Testament were associated with the following events:

- **The Sabbath** – Saturday Old Testament observance as the mandated day for rest and worship (Leviticus 23:3).

- **The Passover and Festival of Unleavened Bread** – Passover was held on the fourteenth day of the first month (usually somewhere around March or April), and the Festival of Unleavened bread began on the fifteenth day of that month (usually somewhere between March and April). For seven days, the Israelites were forbidden from eating any bread with leaven (yeast). In that period, they were to present a food offering to the Lord, and on the seventh day, they held a sacred assembly and were forbidden from doing any ordinary labor (Leviticus 23:4-8).

- **Offering of the Firstfruits** – Held at the end of the grain harvest when the firstfruits offering of the grain was brought to the priests and offered to the Lord on the day after the Sabbath (Sunday). It is turned into a cake and presented with wine. When observing this feast, they were not to eat any bread, roasted grain, or new grain until the offering was brought before God (Leviticus 23:9-14).

- **The Festival of Weeks** – Held fifty days after the Offering of the Firstfruits; we have come to associate this feast with Pentecost in Christianity. It was a harvest festival, offering new grain (brought forth in the form of two loaves of bread), seven male lambs without defect, one young bull, two rams, and a drink offering. The various items were brought forth for sacrifice: one for firstfruits, one as a sin offering, one as a fellowship offering, one as a wave offering, and all as a sacred offering. That same day, a sacred assembly was called and no one was to do ordinary labor (Leviticus 23:15-22).

- **The Festival of Trumpets** – Held on the first day of the seventh month (somewhere between September and October) as a day of "Sabbath rest" not held on the actual Sabbath. The sacred assembly held on this day began with trumpet blasts and required a food offering to God and complete rest from all labor (Leviticus 23:23-25).

- **The Day of Atonement** – The holiest day on the Hebrew calendar, held on the tenth day of the seventh month (somewhere between September and October), this day required a sacred assembly, complete fast, and a food offering to God. Those who did not fast and did not follow the regulations were to be cut off from the people. It was a required Sabbath when the High Priest would enter the Holy of Holies to atone for the sins of Israel (Leviticus 23:26-32).

- **The Festival of Tabernacles** – Held on the fifteenth day of the seventh month (between September and October), lasting for seven days. The first day is a sacred assembly, requiring rest from all regular work. Food offerings are made to the Lord and on the eighth day, a sacred assembly is held again where food offerings are made (Leviticus 23:33-36).

- **Purim** – The Feast of Purim celebrates the heroic work of Queen Esther, whose intervention ensured the Jews were not eradicated through genocide, desired by Haman, under the reign of King Xeres of Persia (Esther 9:20-26).

- **National festival** – Called by a governmental leader to celebrate something specific or handle something specific (1 Kings 8:5-65, 1 Chronicles 28:8-29:20).

- **General repentance** – Solemn assemblies called so the people would seek God, repent, and change their ways (Joel 1:14-2:16).

Sacred assemblies in the New Testament were associated with the following events:

- **Pentecost** – The gathering of the disciples at Jerusalem, awaiting instructions from the Lord, transformed the entire understanding of Pentecost forever. Frequently spoken of as the birthday of the church, Pentecost teaches the church to be the firstfruits of the

Lord, those that the Lord seeks to transform unto salvation. On the feast of Pentecost, the Holy Spirit descended upon the disciples and each spoke in other tongues, in what we often speak of as the gift of tongues or the baptism of the Holy Spirit. Each individual heard whatever was spoken in their own native language. The Apostle Peter then stood up and addressed a large gathering of Jews from every nation to explain the gift of tongues and to provide all present with the opportunity to hear the Gospel of Jesus Christ, repent, and be water baptized. As a result, thousands of souls were saved and the believers came together, uniting and having all things in common (Acts 2:1-47).

- **Communion** – Even though communion was held as a general practice as a part of weekly services or regular church gatherings, communion was held in a high respect and observed as a special assembly, a special time and a special service (1 Corinthians 11:17-34)

- **Council gathering at Jerusalem** – The early church had its issues, and one of the primary ones was whether or not someone could be a Christian without first becoming Jewish. In order to discuss this issue, the apostles and elders met to consider the issue and walked away with the understanding that there was no reason why the Gentiles needed to first become Jewish in order to join God's assembly and follow Christ. Their advice was, instead, to abstain from food polluted by idols, avoid sexual immorality, and avoid the meat of strangled animals and blood. The result of this gathering was a letter, which was circulated among the churches (Acts 15:1-35).

I show this list to prove that assemblies and special events were added to, changed, and modified over time as new issues came to light and people desired to celebrate the new things God had done for them. While we might celebrate the new things of God and may no longer observe the older ones because they type and shadow of what they prefigured has now come, there is nothing wrong with the principle of celebration and gathering together for sacred purpose.

WHY A CHAPTER ON GRADUATION SERVICES AND SACRED ASSEMBLIES TOGETHER?

Mighty gates: lift up your heads! Ancient doors: rise up high!
So the glorious king can enter! Who is this glorious king?
The LORD—strong and powerful! The LORD—powerful in battle!
- Psalm 24:7-8 (CEB)

Graduation services and sacred assemblies are both special services that are held at a specific and designated time for a specific purpose. Because both revolve around group gatherings and individual elevations much of the time, they have many things in common in their structure and execution. Since their general format is similar, we are looking at both as one chapter.

CELEBRATING WHAT GOD IS DOING WITHIN, THROUGH, AND AMONG US

But ye are come unto mount Sion, and unto the city of the living God, the heavenly Jerusalem,
and to an innumerable company of angels, To the general assembly and church of the firstborn,
which are written in heaven, and to God the Judge of all, and to the spirits of just men made perfect,
And to Jesus the mediator of the new covenant, and to the blood of sprinkling, that speaketh better things
than that of Abel.
- Hebrews 12:22-24

In Biblical times, they did not observe many of the specific graduation services that we see acknowledged now. Their cultures were different and many of the social observations that we see in our cultures (such as birthdays and anniversaries) were either not observed or not regarded as sacred celebrations. They did have sacred assemblies, and they did dedicate buildings, but we don't see birthday services, watchnight service, pastoral anniversaries, or program completion classes in church. It's also worth mentioning that the sacred assemblies and building dedications were far different from the way we recognize them today. For this reason, some argue that such ceremonies are unbiblical and we should not observe them.

Even though the category of graduation services and sacred assemblies as we understand them today are not always for specified Biblical observances, that does not mean what is done within them is unbiblical or improper for Christians. The Bible does tell us that we should not forsake the assembling of ourselves together (Hebrews 10:24-25) and it also states we should honor those who have rule among us (Hebrews 13:7, Hebrews 13:17, Hebrews 13:24). There are many places where the Bible instructs us to lift one another up and to encourage one another (Romans 14:19, 1 Corinthians 14:12, 1 Corinthians 14:26, Ephesians 4:16, Ephesians 4:29, 1 Thessalonians 5:11). Just because the specific title of each of these events does not have Biblical mention or because the way they are done now has been modernized does not mean that they are inapplicable or spiritually null and void. If anything, the purposes found in graduation services and sacred assemblies teach us much about the Kingdom and Kingdom life beyond our own immediate understandings:

- **Kingdom of God within** – The Bible teaches us that the Kingdom of God is within, around, and among us (Luke 17:20-21). It's not just about "us and Jesus," it's about us getting right with Jesus so that we can live the Kingdom in celebration with others. When we celebrate what God is doing for ourselves and others or we celebrate what God is doing within a Kingdom organization, we come to a greater understanding of what God wants to do in the church and in us as individuals.

- **We are the Kingdom** – The Kingdom of God is not far off and distant, somewhere unobtainable (Matthew 3:1-3). The Kingdom is us; we are the Kingdom, in the Kingdom, and of the Kingdom. We like to talk about Kingdom, but we don't always like to be a part of the Kingdom or live the Kingdom. Gathering together to acknowledge others or to come together as one organization, one Body in Christ (1 Corinthians 12:1-31).

- **We are family** – The church today likes the idea of nuclear family values (husbands and wives, children and parents). We don't often consider that, as Christians we are also family (Ephesians 2:1-22). We are brothers and sisters in the Lord. Even though our positions in the church may be different, God is still our Father and we are His sons and daughters, working together, and learning about love and getting along with others in our big extended family.

- **We are a chosen generation** – The first Christians were a chosen generation in that they were the first to experience the church experience after the resurrection of Jesus. We are now a generation that has been chosen to leave its mark on this generation, in this time, and in this season. God has not placed us here by accident (Esther 4:14). When we come together and celebrate what He is doing within our lives, whether it's because He has graced us to see another year or because we have ordinations to handle, He has established us in this generation and that is something to celebrate as we stand strong and firm in this era of history.

- **We are a royal priesthood** – The priesthood of all believers sometimes loses its special and important ring when we say it so much to try and prove a counterpoint against another spiritual or religious group. We are royal because we are the children of the King (Romans 8:14-17, Galatians 3:29, Galatians 4:6) and established as a priesthood means we are here to present Christ's sacrifice to the world, as His diligent workers.

- **We are a peculiar people** – Once we become a part of the Kingdom, our priorities change. We don't desire to turn it up in a nightclub any longer or to celebrate our birthdays at a bar. Being peculiar means how we celebrate our milestones change and it means that our fellowship changes, as well (John 14:17, 1 John 2:15-16). This doesn't mean you can't have friends who are not Christian, but it does mean that when it comes to special occasions, we want to celebrate them with God and our family in Christ.

THE IMPORTANCE OF COMING TOGETHER AS ONE

And let us consider one another to provoke unto love and to good works: Not forsaking the assembling of ourselves together, as the manner of some is; but exhorting one another: and so much the more, as ye see the day approaching.
- Hebrews 10:24-25

I believe that we have a serious disconnect when it comes to unity in the church today. We say we love God and we love each other, but it's not uncommon to meet believers who never interact or fellowship with others beyond their immediate local church. This is a new phenomenon, because in years past, churches were a part of denominations, dioceses, assemblies, and larger groups that connected the local churches together. Most also sponsored missionaries who went to other countries or different regions to work and then came back to do reports on their experiences overseas. Many of these churches also contributed to missions and missionaries and also sponsored students to attend denomination-sponsored schools for seminary or further study. In addition to these different connections, regional directors often visited local churches and most groups had regional and annual or bi-annual international assemblies for the entire church.

This all means that churches in days prior were not so limited to the idea that they were one local church and that there was no church beyond them. They saw the international church, they touched it, they believed in it, and they experienced it. They were well accustomed to the idea that people belonged to their denomination who looked different from them, spoke different languages, were of different races, and held different social customs. The church wasn't just one church, somewhere, that never went beyond its own doors.

There's nothing wrong with needing the reminder that we are many parts, but one Body. I was asked not long ago by a man from Pakistan as to which church is the true church. My explanation to him was not what I would have ordinarily expected to come out of my mouth, but it was true, nonetheless. I pointed out to him that we are many parts in one body, and that means if a church is truly following its mandate from the Lord, then they are all a part of that one body. The Body of Christ goes beyond one church, one ministry, one denomination. We all have specific assignments to complete, and those are not always clearly completed in one specific location. It takes all of us, working together, working in agreement, and working in unity to bring that to pass.

This means that our graduation services that bring in local community members and churches and our sacred assemblies that bring in churches connected to one another all throughout the world remind us that there is one body, one Spirit, one hope, one Lord, one faith, one baptism, one God and Father of all, Who is above all, and through and in all (Ephesians 4:4-6). Sacred assemblies, graduation services, and all occasions that draw believers together remind us that we are all one, striving toward all God desires us to become.

PREPARATION FOR GRADUATION SERVICES AND SACRED ASSEMBLIES

And Moses did as the Lord commanded him; and the assembly was gathered together unto the door of the tabernacle of the congregation.
- Leviticus 8:4

The preparations involved in these special services involve the work of multiple people in a ministry or international assembly. Because they are community or international services, they don't just happen by accident. Depending on the nature of the service, preparations may start with a committee appointed to oversee the project's function either weeks or months in advance. Many international assemblies start planning year-to-year in advance. Discussion of preparation for whatever the service may be should start within a church or ministry meeting, first of the board, and then a general meeting that discusses who will do want and what is needed to do what. In order to prepare an event from a reasonable perspective, the following should be considered:

- **The event theme** – Not all events have themes, but it can be useful to set the atmosphere and tone of an event, and to move forward with the planning.

- **The event budget** – I believe in faith but I also know the realities of event planning, and events of all sorts – even local ones – can be very expensive. While yes, we believe in the Lord to provide, we still need to be reasonable about what we can afford for an event and remember that there are many things that go into making a church or ministry function. It's not reasonable to sink all the expenses a ministry has into event overhead when there are practical things, such as rent, outreach, materials, and so many other things that we need to cover. Budgeting events ensures there will be money for everything in the bigger picture as well as pulling off a powerful event.

- **Meeting spaces** – Sometimes churches or regular meeting spaces are not large enough for the anticipated crowds, especially when the crowd includes people who are not members of the church. The balance of selecting something not too large and not too small can be tricky, but it is a good reason to encourage registration, RSVP, or some form of communication with attendees so a reasonable head count can be estimated when it's time to reserve a space. If there is a large number of people travelling from out of town, it is within the order of the event to establish a room block, affording them reasonable group rates, for the duration of their stay.

- **The spiritual preparations involved for the leadership** – If you are hosting a sacred assembly of sorts, the leadership involved that will oversee the event needs to delegate smaller tasks to those who can handle them so they have the freedom to prepare spiritually. There are numerous spiritual preparations that must be covered before a large event begins, and the only way things can be within spiritual order is if the leaders involved take the necessary time to focus in and hear from the Lord as to the general direction the event should take.

- **Preparations for those who will be celebrated or receiving rites** – If the ceremony involves celebration of a person, ordination, appointment, or some other celebration, the individual or individuals should be prepared prior to the event.

- **Advertising** – Events should always feature an event flyer that contains title of event, date and time, location, and featured speakers or some general content about the event itself. If an event is strictly within a ministry or organization, the event should be advertised with plenty of time to plan one's attendance.

- **Event agenda** – Even the simplest of events should have some sort of format to follow. First preaching ceremonies, birthday services and pastoral anniversaries should have an order of service. Convocations and conferences should map out events for the entire duration, and things should be planned and prepared, decently and in order.

- **Post-event considerations** – Most events rate feedback, photos or videos for individuals who could not attend, clean-up, organization, and budget reporting. Leaders and assistants who have helped bring the event to fruition will, most likely, also be quite tired and not physically or spiritually ready to jump into life as they know it, so trips and preaching engagements should be scheduled around large events. Always consider the post-event work as much as you would consider preparations.

MINISTER PRESENTATION

Praise ye the Lord. I will praise the Lord with my whole heart, in the assembly of the upright, and in the congregation.
- Psalm 111:1

Most graduation services and sacred assemblies are considered solemn occasions. The few exceptions to this would be a birthday or pastoral anniversary service and holiday services if a group observes them. These specific instances would warrant attire and conduct as is specified by the church or ministry holding them, and it is usually acceptable for anyone attending to come in regular Sunday clothes or church dress. Convocation or other sacred assembly, group ordination or minister's ordination may require more formalized ceremonial wear, including a collar and shirt, robe, or other clothing outlined for formal occasions. There may be different attires required for different convocation or assembly activities, and all participants should take note of proper attire as is required.

CEREMONY

Different graduation services and sacred assemblies have different ceremonial components to them, but here, I am going to give a sample service for a graduation service and then an outline for a sample sacred assembly. These ceremonies have complete flexibility and there is no reason not to shake things up, move them around, or modify as needed.

Graduation Service:

- Introduction and welcome

- Praise and Worship

- Prayer

- Offering

- Special musical or dance selection

- Introduction of the speaker

- Speaker's message

- Special selection

- Presentation of gifts, papers, or celebration for the event

- Tribute to the leader or event

- Final remarks

- Closing announcements

- Dismissal with prayer, song, or both

Sacred Assembly:

Day 1

- Meet and greet

- Intercessory prayer

- Leadership meeting

- Evening service

Day 2

- Morning prayer

- Children and youth activities

- General assembly meeting

- Minister's luncheon

- Afternoon seminars

- Rest/fellowship

- Evening service

Day 3

- Morning prayer

- Convocation assembly service

- Assembly ordination service

- Leadership retreat service

- Group dismissal

GRADUATION SERVICES AND SACRED ASSEMBLIES DOS AND DON'TS:

- DO embrace the idea of graduation services and sacred assemblies as an opportunity to live out Kingdom virtue, celebrate one another, honor leadership, and to display fellowship within the church.
- DO take the opportunity to gather together as a display of unity, truth, oneness, and purpose in the Body of Christ.
- DO see such events as an opportunity to live and display Kingdom in a deeper way.
- DO plan events well, taking as much time as needed, and consider all essentials of good planning, space, preparation, advertising agenda, finances, and post-event considerations.
- DO dress appropriately, making sure to consider the appropriate attire of the event itself or the events within the event.

- DON'T ignore sacred assemblies and graduation services because they don't fall within the guidelines of what is traditional.
- DON'T miss the relevance of the universal church present in such events.
- DON'T ignore the planning process involved in such events.

- DON'T forget to set up an order of service or event agenda to keep the flow of such events running smoothly and purposed.

SECTION II

RITUALS

STAINED-GLASS WINDOW DEPICTION OF A BABY DEDICATION

CHAPTER SIX

PRESENTATIONS/DEDICATIONS

And when the days of her purification according to the law of Moses were accomplished, they brought Him to Jerusalem, to present Him to the Lord; (As it is written in the law of the LORD, Every male that openeth the womb shall be called holy to the Lord;) And to offer a sacrifice according to that which is said in the law of the Lord, A pair of turtledoves, or two young pigeons.
- Luke 2:22-24

WHAT IS A PRESENTATION/DEDICATION?

Lord, now lettest Thou thy servant depart in peace, according to Thy word: For mine eyes have seen Thy salvation, Which Thou hast prepared before the face of all people; A light to lighten the Gentiles, and the glory of Thy people Israel. And Joseph and his mother marvelled at those things which were spoken of Him.
- Luke 2:29-33

A dedication service (also called a presentation service) is a simple, joyful ceremony when one presents their child before the church and dedicates that child to God. The rite of dedication was done on behalf of Jesus by His parents after His birth (Luke 2:25-32). We also see the practice done throughout the Old Testament (Exodus 13:1, 1 Samuel 1:24-28). In Old Testament times, it was done on firstborn children, especially males, and children of promise, who had a specific purpose for the Lord. Now we recognize every child to have a purpose of the Lord, whatever His purpose for them may be. As we recognize this ceremony was full of promise, prophecy, and evangelism, so too we continue this legacy with our own children, born into faith and promise, today. This birth into our faith and promise can come about by natural birth, or by adoption, depending on the circumstances of the parents and children involved.

SHOULD WE DO PRESENTATIONS?

For I know him, that he will command his children and his household after him, and they shall keep the way of the LORD, to do justice and judgment; that the LORD may bring upon Abraham that which He hath spoken of him.
- Genesis 18:19

Dedication used to be done by the majority of Christian churches, both denominational and non-denominational. In recent years, the practice has faded and is not as common as it once was.

Some argue the presentation practice serves as a replacement for infant baptism. Since it is not baptism, and the practice comes from the Bible, there is no justification to support it is a replacement for something else.

A dedication is an entrusting of faith. All a dedication does is ask God to bless a child and the parents, godparents (if there are any), and the general community make the commitment to see to it that the child will be raised in the faith. This lays the foundation for a child to choose the Lord when they are of the appropriate age of decision later on.

Dedications can be an important step for parents and an important establishment for the community. It takes more than parents to raise a child: it takes a Christian community and the Kingdom of God working together to continue the faith. There is nothing unbiblical about a presentation, nor is presentation required. A dedication should be performed if the parents desire it to be done, but should not be forced upon them. It is an option that should be given, and should be celebrated.

WHY ARE DEDICATIONS IMPORTANT?

Hear, O Israel: The LORD our God is one LORD: And thou shalt love the LORD thy God with all thine heart, and with all thy soul, and with all thy might. And these words, which I command thee this day, shall be in thine heart: And thou shalt teach them diligently unto thy children, and shalt talk of them when thou sittest in thine house, and when thou walkest by the way, and when thou liest down, and when thou risest up.
- Deuteronomy 6:4-7

Jesus encouraged the children to come to Him, for the Kingdom of heaven belonged to such like them (Matthew 19:14, Luke 18:15-17). Dedications remind us and encourage us in a few basic things:

- The importance of raising children in the faith, both by example and instruction.

- That the church should welcome children, giving them a place and resource that reaches them on their level, teaching them about the Lord, and encouraging them to reach out to God in a way they can understand on their appropriate age level.

- The reminder that we need to be as children in our faith and trust of God.

- That it takes the entire community of faith to raise a child up in the way they should go, and we should not ignore the household of faith's role in raising a child right.

- The cycles of prophecy and faith are circular, not linear. Faith and the hope of faith is beyond our immediate age and generation, and we are called to prepare future generations for their call and task that lies ahead.

REQUESTS FOR PRESENTATION

Tell ye your children of it, and let your children tell their children, and their children another generation.
- Joel 1:3

Presentations are done at the request of the parents. Dedications should be planned shortly after a child joins a family. Children are typically infants during presentations, but in the case of adoptions or members joining the church later, a dedication can be done up to the age of three.

WHAT IS NEEDED FOR DEDICATION?

But Jesus said, Suffer little children, and forbid them not, to come unto Me: for of such is the kingdom of heaven.
- Matthew 19:14

Dedications are simple services that are often done either at the beginning or end of a Sunday service or another service done by the church. It is important the church community is present. Unlike other rites, you do not need additional things to draw on symbolism, save the Word of God. To do a dedication, you need the child, the parents or guardians, and the godparents, if the parents desire to have them.

LET THE CHILDREN COME TO ME

And He shall turn the heart of the fathers to the children, and the heart of the children to their fathers...
- Malachi 4:6

I've heard it said for the past twenty years that parents are concerned about involving their children with organized religion. They desire, instead, to allow children to make their own decisions about God and faith when they are older, and insist that they should raise their child to be spiritually neutral. This probably sounds noble and good on the surface, especially to someone who was raised in a group that they later abandoned because they felt forced to attend. It's true that many of us grew up in churches that were not accurate and we lived by their precepts against our will, because they were what we were taught. Once we reached a certain age, we abandoned those ideals and traded them in for others.

I think it's worth examining if this type of ideal is a good one to have, especially if you have parents who are concerned about harming their child by dedicating them to God. There are a few things that we need to consider about a "religious neutral" upbringing, however. Nobody, no matter how much they might claim to be, is actually "neutral" when it comes to spiritual matters. We all have an opinion, and our ideals and concepts about spiritual things are passed on to our children, no matter how much we might hope they won't. If we give our children the idea that spirituality is something to avoid, that may very well become the thing that follows them through life instead of the solid ideals of faith. As parents and guardians, we want to show children that God is as much theirs as He is ours, and give them a sense of community, involvement, and experience with God for themselves as we would desire for ourselves. It's worth realizing that even though what we might have come from might not be where we are now, it did help form and make us who we are. It wasn't that we were raised in faith that was bad, it was the faith we were raised in, and how much better would your life had been had you been raised in the faith that edifies and encourages you? It's important to seek to give that to your children, to allow them to explore the sacred things, to know them, and to start by seeing to it that they are dedicated to God and presented before your faith community.

Involving children in the faith is a powerful way that families come together. By dedicating children to the Lord, it entrusts God with their future. It makes us more aware of God's providence in our own lives, the need to surrender control, and our need to trust God, all the more, realizing that we are, before Him, all as children.

IMPORTANCE IN CHILDREN'S PROGRAMS WITHIN THE CHURCH

For the promise is unto you, and to your children, and to all that are afar off, even as many as the LORD our God shall call.
- Acts 2:39

Sometimes we, especially as church leaders, forget about the relevance in Sunday school, children's church, and children's ministries because we focus so much on getting new members or maintaining the ones we have, we don't think about the needs of children in our churches. Children are not adults, and the specific needs they have require that they are taught differently than adults. A Sunday morning service designed and geared for adults will, most likely, lose the attention and interest of a child, and that means churches need to consider the needs of their young members. If Jesus calls the children to Him, that means they are a part of church as much as anyone else is, and we cannot ignore their needs. Churches should have, as needed:

- Sunday school (all ages)
- Children's church
- Youth programs
- Age-appropriate Bible study
- Children and youth services
- Vacation Bible School
- Opportunity for youth to be involved in the various ministries of the church, such as music, dance, ushers, prayer, etc.

WHAT ARE GODPARENTS?

Come, ye children, hearken unto me: I will teach you the fear of the LORD.
- Psalm 34:11

Godparents are individuals selected by the parents or guardians of a child to serve the role of spiritual guidance in the lives of their children. Godparents are typically selected for ceremonial reasons, but should be people whom the parents trust, are well-equipped to stand as spiritual guides, and people who will be involved with the child throughout their lives. Godparents can be a married couple, or two individual people.

WHO CAN PERFORM A PRESENTATION CEREMONY?

But the mercy of the LORD is from everlasting to everlasting upon them that fear Him,
and His righteousness unto children's children.
- Psalm 103:17

Presentation ceremonies are typically performed by ministers. As the presentation ceremony is a special observance for a local church community, it would most often be done by a pastor. In the case of a dedication done for a leader's family (such as an apostle or prophet or other leader that is often itinerant), the ceremony can be done by the leader themselves, or by a leader or associate of the leader.

Simply put, any validly ordained and licensed minister can perform a dedication/presentation ceremony. In this specific case, as was pointing out above, the minister selected to perform this rite should have a relationship with the minister, acknowledging their leadership, and celebrating in this ceremony with them.

MINISTER PRESENTATION

Children's children are the crown of old men; and the glory of children are their fathers.
- Proverbs 17:6

The presiding minister of a dedication should look the part. The occasion is a joyful, formal event. A minister should dress in their typical Sunday or service clothing: a suit or dress, or shirt and collar and robe. The service is an extension of a larger one, providing a special time for this ceremony.

Ministers should provide a dedication/presentation to the parents or guardians, complete with the child's name, date, and signature of the minister, commemorating the occasion.

DEDICATION PREPARATION

Her children arise up, and call her blessed; her husband also, and he praiseth her.
- Proverbs 31:28

Preparation for a dedication service is far simpler than for many other rites within the church. The presiding minister should have a short meeting with the couple or guardians requesting dedication to work out the date and time. The minister should also tell them the significance of dedication and the importance of sharing this with the community at large.

CEREMONY

Presentation should be done one of three ways:

- Before a service.

- After a church service.

- At some point in time during a church service, such as after worship or after the sermon.

The child, family, and any applicable godparents or friends should be invited to come to the front of the church. The minister should give a brief introduction about the ceremony and its significance, and follow with a Scripture reading. Some suggestions include:

- Deuteronomy 6:4-7
- Psalm 127:1-5
- Psalm 139:1-17
- Matthew 19:13-15
- Luke 2:22-40
- Luke 18:15-17

- **Minister:** We come here together to celebrate the dedication of (child's name) _____. As the Lord has told us, "Let the children come to Me," we know this child is special to the Lord, purposed and destined for His purposes, even before the foundation of the world. As this child is special to the Lord, this child, too, is special to all of us: we recognize and embrace their unique gifts, talents, and callings. In the birth of this child, the Lord gave a gift and promise to His Kingdom: and here today, we welcome that promise among the Body of Christ.

- **Minister to the parents/guardians and godparents:** _____ and _____, and _____ and _____, do you promise, as far as you are able, to work together to rear up this child in the ways of the Lord, as a blessing unto your family and the Body of Christ?

- **Parents/guardians:** We do.

- **Minister to the parents/guardians and godparents:** _____ and _____ and _____ and

_____, do you promise, as far as you are able, to develop the gifts and talents of this child, to embrace his/her calling, and to encourage and edify this child to become all God has for them to be?

- **Parents/guardians and godparents:** We do.

- **Minister to the parents, godparents, and congregation:** As the Body of Christ, representative here, do you solemnly promise to support this family in the spiritual development of this child, in love and encouragement, and to be a resource, recognizing God's family extends beyond natural bounds, thereby making all of us one family, united in Christ?

- **Everyone:** We do.

- **Minister to the parents, godparents, and the congregation:** Thus this day, do you all solemnly commit to this child, the commitments of Deuteronomy 6:4-7: to train this child to love the Lord God, with all heart, soul, and might; and to teach His words to this child, talking about them sitting at home, walking on the road, when lying down, and when rising up?

- **Everyone:** We do.

Minister lays hands on child's head.

- **Minister:** Lord, we ask for Your blessing on Your child, (name) _____. May he/she live long in the land, dedicated and focused on You.

Minister takes the child, holds him or her up, and makes the following pronouncement.

- **Minister:** *For this child I prayed; and the LORD hath given me my petition which I asked of Him: Therefore also I have lent him to the LORD; as long as he liveth he shall be lent to the LORD.*

  I present to you all, this child, dedicated to the Lord, (name) _____.

Minister then presents certificate of dedication to the family.

DEDICATION/PRESENTATION DOS AND DON'TS:

- DO support the celebration of life and continuation of the church through dedications and presentations.
- DO meet with the parents who request a dedication.
- DO encourage parents to develop faith in their children and to participate in the spiritual life of the church.
- DO maintain children's programs for your church, ensuring children have a place and a voice within the congregation, relating to them on a level they can understand.
- DO dedication services up to about the age of three years of age.
- DO encourage the parents to select godparents.
- DO dedication/presentations during regular services, so the entire congregation may be involved.
- DO present well, dressing appropriately, and carrying yourself appropriately.

- DON'T force dedications and presentations upon parents.
- DON'T make a dedication service extravagant or overdone.
- DON'T ignore the symbolism present in dedications and presentations.

CONSECRATION PERIOD

CHAPTER SEVEN

CONSECRATION

And ye shall not go out of the door of the tabernacle of the congregation
in seven days, until the days of your consecration be at an end:
for seven days shall he consecrate you.
- Leviticus 8:33

WHAT IS CONSECRATION?

And there was one Anna, a prophetess, the daughter of Phanuel, of the tribe of Aser: she was of a great age,
and had lived with an husband seven years from her virginity; And she was a widow of about fourscore and four
years, which departed not from the temple, but served God with fastings and prayers night and day.
And she coming in that instant gave thanks likewise unto the Lord, and spake of Him to all them that looked for
redemption in Jerusalem.
- Luke 2:36-38

A consecration is a solemn dedication to a special spiritual purpose or task. It can be in the form of dedicating a person to the service of God or a specific service of God, items for God's use, or a period of time devoted to that service or purpose. In the Old Testament, consecration was a general part of the Israelite life. Priests, prophets, Nazarites, objects, and holy men and women of God purposed themselves for God's service through consecration.

Consecration was not a foreign concept in the New Testament, contrary to what some teach. When Mary received the news of Jesus' birth, her visit to Elizabeth proved to be a consecration experience (Luke

1:39-56). The Prophetess Anna, the widow who was the first to tell others about Jesus Christ, consecrated herself unto the Lord, and lived in a state of constant consecration (Luke 2:36-38). The period of time Jesus spent in the desert in fast and prayer was akin to consecration, preparing for His ministry purpose (Matthew 4:1-11). The Apostle Paul also went through a period of consecration, taking a Nazarite vow (Acts 18:18, Acts 21:23-27).

Today most understand consecration as the act of setting one's self apart for the Lord. It is the committed, purposed action to God's service and will in one's life. A consecration may be done by an individual or a group for some dedicated or specific purpose. In both cases, the church may be called on to share in the consecration of the individual or the group.

Consecration is also understood today as being a time of spiritual preparation for that purpose, training, fasting, prayer, or understanding to walk in God's specific purpose or calling. In this understanding, consecration does not just include the work itself, but the preparations and understanding to do God's work, as well.

SHOULD WE OBSERVE CONSECRATION?

Then Paul took the men, and the next day purifying himself with them entered into the temple, to signify the accomplishment of the days of purification, until that an offering should be offered for every one of them. And when the seven days were almost ended, the Jews which were of Asia, when they saw him in the temple, stirred up all the people, and laid hands on him.
- Acts 21:26-27

If you do a search on the internet about consecration for Christians, you will find a variety of opinions. One of the major arguments against consecration for Christians is the stance that every Christian is already set apart for the Lord, and, therefore, consecration is unnecessary. You will also find voices who think people should hold consecration for every area of their lives, ranging from starting a new job to discovering they are having a baby.

I think the truth of the matter lies somewhere in-between the two extremes presented here. Yes, we do understand that Christians are called to be a holy people, set apart for the Lord, but we also need to acknowledge that not everyone – in fact, all of us – do not live up to the standards of holiness that we should. Consecration acknowledges a re-dedication for people to commit themselves to the Lord in a way they should, stepping out in faith and trust, coming before the Lord and seeking His revelation about important matters.

Any Christian who believes in any semblance of rite and ritual: baptism, ordination, baby dedication, etc., already acknowledges the rite of Christian consecration. All of these actions are consecrations of sort: they are setting apart the individuals in them for God's service and purpose. Consecration, in a general sense, doesn't limit the concept to only certain callings or purposes pertaining to the Kingdom, but allows anyone the opportunity to set themselves apart for whatever God is calling them to do. It shows forth their commitment and intention to say "Yes, Lord" in everything they do for Him.

Modern leaders constantly complain that people today do not understand the importance of commitment and purpose. If we understand consecration as one's decision to follow God's will and, in the process, make a deeper commitment to Him and His purpose, there is no reason we should ever discourage consecration. If anything, it is something we should encourage.

At the same time, we must remain balanced in our perspective about consecration. We don't need to do a consecration for every little thing. People who believe they should do consecrations to get a new car, are starting a new job, or want to move into a new apartment have missed the purpose of consecration. This means it is very important for leaders to teach on consecration, consecrated purpose, and raise up the relevance of holiness and dedication to the Lord in His ways and purposes, rather than those of our own.

In summary, consecration is both a reminder and a preparation. It sets us to spiritual things, for spiritual things, and is yet another way we can show our commitment to the Lord in a deeper way. We should encourage consecration as the Lord leads, and educate on what it is and its importance in the lives of believers as leaders in the faith.

WHY IS CONSECRATION IMPORTANT?

Wherefore, my beloved, as ye have always obeyed, not as in my presence only, but now much more in my absence,
work out your own salvation with fear and trembling.
- Philippians 2:12

Consecration is important because it is a time of new or renewed focus. It is, in a sense, another repentance in our lives: it is turning ourselves to God's ways. Maybe it is not in the big sense of initial conversion, but it is an alignment with Him along the way as we work out our salvation with fear and trembling (Philippians 2:12). Consecration reminds us all of the continued call to holiness; to re-evaluate where we are and make that much of a better effort to become who God calls us to be; and to focus that much more on what God has called each one of us to do.

Lastly, consecration is important because it reminds us all that the focus, dedication, and discipline of consecration should be applied to our lives as we walk with Christ. It is so easy to be distracted away from the things of God today. Many of these distractions come from people in the church themselves who lead us to believe the ultimate happiness lies in money, a relationship, being famous, in having a big ministry, or in something other than the Lord God Himself. Following these pursuits, even if it is only for a period of time, requires us to go back to the basics, hear from the Lord, and learn what He is truly saying and calling in the midst of worldly problems, misunderstanding, falsehood, and chaos.

CIRCUMSTANCES FOR CONSECRATION

But if from thence thou shalt seek the LORD thy God, thou shalt find Him,
if thou seek Him with all thy heart and with all thy soul.
- Deuteronomy 4:29

As was stated earlier, consecration is not appropriate for every circumstance. The proper circumstances for consecration dictate three possible situations:

- A major shift in someone's life, such as answering a calling from the Father, changing direction in a ministry or situation in their life.

- For those who have received a directive from God and require a time of seeking God deeper, for clarity, perspective, and preparation.

- For a specific event, such as preparation for a church revival, conference, etc., or something personal, such as a wedding or vocational station.

CALLING TO CONSECRATION

Hearken to me, ye that follow after righteousness, ye that seek the LORD: look unto the rock whence ye are hewn, and to the hole of the pit whence ye are digged.
- Isaiah 51:1

The call to consecration comes from God. In the natural realm, a consecration is either called by an individual or a community/ministry leader. The individual may make a personal call to consecration, spending additional time in the Lord, or going about life as usual. They may also take what is commonly called a "sabbatical," devoting a specified period of time to the direction, guidance, and preparation for God's task ahead.

If an individual is called to consecration, they may speak of it to others, or they may not. They may go to their leader, seeking confirmation, or may want a formal ceremony of consecration. When a person hears the call to consecration, what God may place on their heart to commemorate the call may be different. Leaders need to be open and aware, and willing to work and support, as they move in their call of consecration.

In the case of a group preparation for an event, the leader would call the congregation or community to a period of consecration. An announcement would be made at a service or via a communication method, complete with the dates for the consecration period.

THE PERIOD OF CONSECRATION

Seek Him that maketh the seven stars and Orion, and turneth the shadow of death into the morning, and maketh the day dark with night: that calleth for the waters of the sea, and poureth them out upon the face of the earth: The LORD is His Name.
- Amos 5:8

As a rule, the specifics of consecration depend on the preparation at hand. A leader might go on consecration for a month, forty days, sixty days, or longer, depending on what is needed. A person spending time in discernment and preparation for a ministry call will do something different during on their consecration than a church member on consecration for souls to attend an upcoming church revival.

For a consecration to be genuine, there are five main points to cover:

- **Seeking God** – A person on consecration will be seeking God in prayer, supplication, and communication with the Most High. This means that, even if during consecration they do not cease regular daily activities (such as working), they will devote additional time to prayer and communication with God, above and beyond what they may normally do.

- **Hearing from God** – One of the main purposes of consecration is to receive God's direction through the Holy Spirit. It's not all about petitioning God, but also about receiving the necessary guidance needed for whatever is next. Nobody should ever walk away from a consecration period without receiving what was necessary to work through in the process.

- **Study** – Study of God's Word is key during consecration. This is the study of the Word beyond a nominative daily reading many believers do. Its purpose is to seek God for the purpose at hand, to which one is called. This study is about hearing from God.

- **Fast** – Fasting is key for consecration. It is important for believers to recognize the fast of consecration is not all about, nor necessarily about, eating. If one is truly seeking to hear from God, they will remove any distractions from their life that may hinder their ability to hear from God. This may include a media fast (television, internet, radio, cell phones), a period of sexual abstinence or a relationship fast, a communication fast (not speaking to certain people for the duration), or the like.

- **Separation** – Consecration is a separation, a separating one's self for the purposes of holiness to the Father and receiving His direction. People on consecration should not be overly social, going out with friends, hanging out, and so on. During consecration, seek the Lord – not distractions.

MINISTER PRESENTATION

For the priest's lips should keep knowledge, and they should seek the law at His mouth:
for He is the messenger of the LORD of hosts.
- Malachi 2:7

A minister should always be supportive of consecration, be it by an individual or a group. If a person does not want their consecration to be made public, the minister should maintain that confidentiality. If an individual desires prayer for a consecration, it should be clarified whether that is done in public or more privately. Private prayer for consecration can be done informally or formally, depending on the individual's wishes. A public consecration ceremony should be done as part of a weekly service and involve the congregation. When done as part of service, the minister should align himself or herself accordingly, in the appropriate service attire.

CONSECRATION PREPARATION

And to this agree the words of the prophets; as it is written, After this I will return, and will build again
the tabernacle of David, which is fallen down; and I will build again the ruins thereof, and I will set it up:
That the residue of men might seek after the Lord, and all the Gentiles, upon whom My Name is called,
saith the Lord, Who doeth all these things.
- Acts 15:15-17

When God calls people to consecration, they should prepare for the consecration period by getting a clear picture of what is asking of them during that time. They may seek leadership guidance, which is where the minister comes into play. If a minister is consulted on consecration, they should encourage and guide in the process as needed. In the specific situation of consecration, the leader should allow themselves to step back and allow God to guide the individual, intervening as asked, and offering advice as necessary.

CEREMONY

A public consecration ceremony is a simple, public event involving confirmation and prayer. The recipient should be dressed appropriately and called to the front of the church, either before or after the service. A brief word should be spoken about the consecration and the congregation asked to pray, followed by the laying on of hands in prayer as a preparation and encouragement for the spiritual time to come.

CONSECRATION DOS AND DON'TS:

- DO recognize periods of time in which people need to seek God more intensely, hear His voice, and receive preparation for the future task at hand.
- DO teach on the correct understanding of consecration, and circumstances therein that warrant it.
- DO teach on the true points of consecration: seeking God, hearing from God, study, fasting, and separation.
- DO support those who go on consecration, and be available for questions and guidance.
- DO have a public consecration ceremony, if such is desired.

- DON'T reduce or distort the concept of consecration.
- DON'T force someone to have a public consecration ceremony if they do not want one.

- DON'T think that just because consecration is desired, that it is properly understood.
- DON'T shut yourself off as a leader from someone just because they are on consecration.

ANOINTING OIL

CHAPTER EIGHT

ANOINTING

Is any sick among you? let him call for the elders of the church; and let them pray over him, anointing him with oil in the Name of the Lord: And the prayer of faith shall save the sick, and the Lord shall raise him up; and if he have committed sins, they shall be forgiven him.
- James 5:14-15

WHAT IS ANOINTING?

> *The LORD is their strength, and He is the saving strength of His anointed.*
> *- Psalm 28:8*

Anointing is the process by which someone or something is smeared with oil for a specific purpose. In the Old Testament, items used for holy purposes were anointed (Genesis 31:13, Exodus 30:26), as were people set apart in the Lord's service, including priests, kings, and prophets (Exodus 28:41, Exodus 29:29, Exodus 40:15, Leviticus 4:3, Psalm 89:20, Isaiah 61:1, Luke 4:18). It was also used to indicate the Lord's protection (1 Chronicles 16:22, Psalm 20:6). We are told in the New Testament that those who are sick should come to the elders in the church for prayer and anointing. If all is done in faith, they shall receive their healing, and shall receive healing for whatever they need healing for.

SHOULD WE DO ANOINTING?

And they cast out many devils, and anointed with oil many that were sick, and healed them.
- Mark 6:13

It's uncommon to see churches follow the protocol for New Testament anointing in modern times. While many will lay hands for healing or as a part of prayer, few churches will anoint someone who comes forth for healing.

The reason for this is simple: many in modern denominations doubt God's ability to heal. Much of the time prayer is regarded as a formality rather than carrying true healing power. As a result of such a mindset, the power of God's healing does not flow because God's order is not present.

Another reason why anointing protocols are not followed is due to modern dependence on medicine and medical intervention. Our society constantly goes running to the doctor with every little problem and every little ailment, which means people do not look to God, nor trust Him, for their healing.

We should do anointing for one reason: because God has appointed the laying on of hands and anointing of the sick for their healing. Ignoring or altering this important command defies God's appointed order for this purpose.

WHY IS ANOINTING IMPORTANT?

Then washed I thee with water; yea, I thoroughly washed away thy blood from thee, and I anointed thee with oil.
- Ezekiel 16:9

In ancient cultures, anointing was as medicinal as it was spiritual. It served as a balm, and signified the refreshing and reinvigorating of the body (Psalm 45:7, Amos 6:6, Matthew 6:17, John 9:6-11). Anointing is a powerful symbol of healing, treatment, wellness, and vigor within the body. Anointing for healing – emotional, physical, mental, and spiritual – is a part of the symbolic hand of God working in someone's life and healing process within God's order.

WHO IS A CANDIDATE TO RECEIVE ANOINTING?

He answered and said, A man that is called Jesus made clay, and anointed mine eyes, and said unto me,
Go to the pool of Siloam, and wash: and I went and washed, and I received sight.
- John 9:11

As leaders, we have no right to turn anyone away who is in need of healing or anointing for any reason. We may not know all the circumstances which surround a need for healing, every little detail, and every dynamic, but if someone comes forth for healing, it is our responsibility as leaders to lay hands and anoint, facilitating God's purpose for divine healing. A candidate for anointing is someone who knows they need healing and comes forward to receive God's opportunity for healing in the anointing, prayer, and laying on of hands.

WHAT IS NEEDED TO DO ANOINTING?

I counsel thee to buy of Me gold tried in the fire, that thou mayest be rich; and white raiment,
that thou mayest be clothed, and that the shame of thy nakedness do not appear;
and anoint thine eyes with eyesalve, that thou mayest see.
- Revelation 3:18

To have an anointing ritual, the following is needed:

- A leader or leaders to do the laying on of hands.

- Anointing oil to anoint the sick and those who come forward. There are a variety of anointing oils available today, all with a different meaning and scent. I do encourage leaders to find an anointing oil for use that does not smell horrific, as some of them do. The available scents today range from traditional Old Testament anointing recipes to other Biblical scent combinations and balms, such as lily of the valley, rose of Sharon, spikenard, and latter rain. Anointing oil is reasonably inexpensive and practical for both local and travel usage.

ANOINTING FORMULA

Thou hast loved righteousness, and hated iniquity; therefore God, even thy God,
hath anointed thee with the oil of gladness above thy fellows.
- Hebrews 1:9

There is no right or wrong way to do an anointing. The essential components are laying on of hands, prayer, and anointing. The only major stipulation is that with all that is done, it is done in faith. The minister has the option to ask about the healing needed or allow the Lord to deliver a word about the needed healing, or both. The only requirement is the Lord has His flow of healing and anointing present in the atmosphere.

WHO CAN PERFORM AN ANOINTING?

Thou preparest a table before me in the presence of mine enemies: Thou anointest my head with oil;
my cup runneth over.
- Psalm 23:5

The Bible stipulates going to the "elders of the church." This can have two understandings. The first is for individuals to go to those who are overseers of the local church in the context of an elder. The second understanding is to go to those who are elders in ministry and in leadership, indicating those who are of acknowledged authority within the church as a whole. Both understandings apply and are beneficial to anointing. The individual who does anointing may be a leader in an immediate church or someone who is visiting with a healing gift. The person who performs the ritual must be a leader, acknowledged within the church. Under no means should someone be allowed to lay hands on individuals with the authorization if they do not have a confirmed gift and some training, as doing such can transfer spirits.

MINISTER PRESENTATION

But my horn shalt Thou exalt like the horn of an unicorn: I shall be anointed with fresh oil.
- Psalm 92:10

There are two circumstances which may surround anointing. The first is a private request to do an anointing. As a minister, it is not uncommon to find needs in people that require both counseling and prayer and anointing. Someone may come forward who desires prayer for a situation and does not want to make the matter public to everyone. Anointing can, and should, be done both as part of service and upon request. In this situation, the minister's presentation may be casual.

In the second circumstance, an anointing ceremony is public. It can be done as its own service or as part of another service, both in a special circumstance or on its own. In these settings, a minister should be in their appropriate service attire. They should be equipped with anointing oil and necessary altar supplies, such as altar cloths and altar workers, to assist if people are slain in the Spirit during the experience. Altar workers should be trained for such times as this by the appropriate leader in order, decency, and proper conduct during this time. Both men and women should be available to "catch" people based on their gender and size and should gently lay the individuals down and cover them with an altar cloth. People should be assisted when getting up, to keep them from tripping on cloths and to help them to their seats or to a seat as necessary. Someone should also assist the minister, holding anointing oil for them, holding items such as a microphone or towel as necessary, and keeping them in prayer as they do powerful warfare in the Spirit.

The minister of God should be very well prepared for anointing and laying on of hands for healing. Deliverance ministry can easily come forth from prayers for healing, and that means a minister may encounter intense and powerful warfare as they deal with spirits that may manipulate, control, or affect the welfare of a person in need of healing. Deliverance and healing often go together, and work in conjunction with one another. Deliverance training is a prophetic training, and involves the discernment of spirits, the process of casting out (which comes through prayer and the laying on of hands), and expected struggles that one may encounter. It's important to keep in mind that deliverance ministry often takes many forms. While some deliverance experiences involve throwing up, shaking, or very dramatic encounters (all of which one should be prepared for), deliverance can also be very quiet and very intense. If a minister is not ready for deliverance ministry, they should partner in healing experiences with a minister who is so as to not encounter anything for which they may be unprepared for. It is also my own personal opinion that, as those in the New Testament were often set out in pairs (Luke 10:1), when it comes to healing and deliverance, having more than one minister present in healing and deliverance situations is best, even if one assists the other. That way, in the event of any circumstance, they are prepared for whatever may come.

CEREMONY

Anointing with laying on of hands does not have a specific formal ceremony, but can be done either privately or as part of service. When done as part of service, be sure to include the following:

- Soft music to play in the background.

- An invitation for healing, extended to everyone in the church or facility.

- Anointing, laying on of hands, and prayer for every individual who comes forward.

- Adequate altar assistance to assist with the ritual.

ANOINTING DOS AND DON'TS:

- DO understand the proper context to anointing.
- DO study anointing, its uses, and why we must anoint for healing in alignment with God's established order.
- DO recognize the importance of anointing.
- DO purchase anointing oil, and have it on hand for any occasion which may arise.
- DO be prepared for healing and deliverance ministry.

- DON'T think anointing is no longer purposed or useful today.

- DON'T turn people away who desire anointing and laying on of hands.
- DON'T select an anointing oil with an overly strong or overpowering smell.
- DON'T be unprepared when it comes to healing and deliverance ministry.
- DON'T feel that you have to handle anointing and deliverance alone.

SECTION III

ORDINANCES

A BAPTISM DONE IN A RIVER

CHAPTER NINE

WATER BAPTISM

There is...One Lord, one faith, one baptism...
- Ephesians 4:4,5

WHAT IS WATER BAPTISM?

John did baptize in the wilderness, and preach the baptism of repentance for the remission of sins.
— Mark 1:4

Baptism is a full immersion in water, symbolic of dying to the old man, in Christ, and then rising to new life in Him. As the Spirit was present at creation, hovering over the water (Genesis 1:1), and thus came forth creation, so the same power is present in baptism, bringing forth new creation from the old life lived to sinful ways.

SHOULD WE DO BAPTISMS?

And he came into all the country about Jordan, preaching the baptism of repentance for the remission of sins.
— Luke 3:3

Many modern denominations – and even some independent ministers – argue against baptism. They say that, for one reason of their own or another, baptism is not needed, that all that matters is one's faith in Christ and that their profession of such faith is a sufficient stand-in for water baptism. Still, others take the opposite approach, believing people have to be baptized in order to be saved. Some take baptism to the extreme, regarding it as the first step of church membership, and baptize everyone, from infancy, because if one is not baptized in water, they cannot be a part of that denomination.

In days gone by, people received the salvation of the Lord and then were taken that very night or morning to the river after service to receive baptism. It was a no-questions asked, none answered part of the salvation process. People who wanted to be baptized were baptized immediately, and there was no question about it. The reason for this is simple: our ancestors recognized the role baptism played in our spiritual process. They did not try to ignore it, redefine it, or intellectualize it beyond what it was. They simply accepted its power in uniting the individual to Christ, burying the individual into His death, and then raising them up to new life in Him.

It's important that, as leaders, we recognize the powerful purpose in baptism. Throughout the New Testament, we hear the command to repent and be baptized (Matthew 3:2, Matthew 3:11, Mark 1:4, Luke 3:3, Acts 19:4). Baptism is a part of the believer's life: it is a part of repentance, of new life, and the symbolic transformation occurring in the individual. Baptism is a part of becoming a new creature in Christ, all things passing away, and new things becoming new, real, and applicable.

The answer as to whether or not we should perform baptisms is unequivocally yes. There is unity present in baptism as one is united to Christ and to the Body of Christ, the church. The question about baptism should not be if we should baptize, but why is the church today questioning the relevance of baptism.

IS BAPTISM A PART OF THE GOSPEL MESSAGE?

For Christ sent me not to baptize, but to preach the gospel: not with wisdom of words,
lest the cross of Christ should be made of none effect.
— 1 Corinthians 1:17

Some today argue that the Apostle Paul denounced baptism when he made his statement found above, in 1 Corinthians 1:17. If we read earlier in the passage, we clearly see that the Apostle Paul was not opposed to baptism, and had even baptized in accordance with his apostolic duty:

Now I beseech you, brethren, by the Name of our Lord Jesus Christ, that ye all speak the same thing, and that there be no divisions among you; but that ye be perfectly joined together in the same mind and in the same judgment. For it hath been declared unto me of you, my brethren, by them which are of the house of Chloe, that there are contentions among you. Now this I say, that every one of you saith, I am of Paul; and I of Apollos; and I of Cephas; and I of Christ. Is Christ divided? was Paul crucified for you? or were ye baptized in the name of Paul? I thank God that I baptized none of you, but Crispus and Gaius; Lest any should say that I had baptized in mine own name. And I baptized also the household of Stephanas: besides, I know not whether I baptized any other.
- I Corinthians 1:10-16

The Apostle Paul was not saying baptism was not a part of the Gospel. He was not denouncing baptism or stating it to be irrelevant. He was not telling people they should not baptize. He himself he had performed baptismal rites in the very passage! What the Apostle Paul was doing here was reasoning with the Corinthian church about divisions over baptism. In ancient culture, it was customary for one to be initiated or affiliated with their teacher into a certain school or understanding of thought. In Corinth, a church heavily influenced by Greek culture, people were being baptized into the names of those in their churches rather than into the Name of Christ. The result was division within the church because people were following men rather than God. The Apostle Paul was using his frustrations over their divisions to teach about two important facets of baptism: baptism into Christ and unity. Baptism is not about uniting ourselves to an earthly leader or teacher, but is about uniting ourselves unto Christ in His death and resurrection. The problem in Corinth was one of misunderstanding the Gospel, and failing to properly propagate it through the rite of baptism. He was establishing his purpose: sent to proclaim the Gospel, not to deal with petty issues. All leaders grow frustrated when the major picture of ministry is promptly halted to deal with smaller, minor issues that people should be past, especially when dealing with them for years in the faith. The Apostle Paul was affirming his call to work unto maturity – not deal with the same issues for years at a time. He wanted to attend to deeper things and expand the Kingdom, not sort out disagreements and vanities.

In keeping, let's look at some Gospel passages pertaining to baptism, affirming baptism as an essential aspect of the Gospel message:

And were baptized of him in Jordan, confessing their sins.
- Matthew 3:6

Then cometh Jesus from Galilee to Jordan unto John, to be baptized of him. But John forbad Him, saying, I have need to be baptized of Thee, and comest Thou to me? And Jesus answering said unto him, Suffer it to be so now: for thus it becometh us to fulfill all righteousness. Then he suffered Him.
- Matthew 3:13-15

And John bare record, saying, I saw the Spirit descending from heaven like a dove, and it abode upon Him. And I knew him not: but He that sent me to baptize with water, the same said unto me, Upon whom thou shalt see the Spirit descending, and remaining on Him, the same is He which baptizeth with the Holy Ghost. And I saw, and bare record that this is the Son of God.
-John 1:32-34

Verily, verily, I say unto thee, except a man be born of water and of the Spirit, he cannot enter into the Kingdom of God.
- John 3:5

Baptism is an essential part of the Gospel because it is both a sign of reception and a unity with the Gospel message. The fruit of reception is found in baptism, as can be found in Acts 2:38-41:

Now when they heard this, they were pricked in their heart, and said unto Peter and to the rest of the apostles, Men and brethren, what shall we do? Then Peter said unto them, Repent, and be baptized every one of you in the Name of Jesus Christ for the remission of sins, and ye shall receive the gift of the Holy Ghost. For the promise is unto you, and to your children, and to all that are afar off, even as many as the LORD our God shall call. And with many other words did he testify and exhort, saying, Save yourselves from this untoward generation. Then they that gladly received his word were baptized: and the same day there were added unto them about three thousand souls.

THE ORIGINS OF BAPTISM

But if we walk in the light, as He is in the light, we have fellowship one with another, and the blood of Jesus Christ His Son cleanseth us from all sin.
I John 1:7

The use of washing for ceremonial cleansing dates back to Old Testament times, particularly within the Mosaic Law (see Leviticus 16). Washing was a common association with spiritual cleansing as well as physical cleansing; however, the use of baptism for the purpose as a sign of repentance is not found within the Old Testament. The connection between the two is found among a group of writings known as The Dead Sea Scrolls. The authors of the Dead Sea Scrolls were a part of an ultra-orthodox, apocalyptic Jewish community living in New Testament times known as the Essenes. In a writing known as *The Manual of Discipline*, the following can be found: *But in a spirit of true counsel for the ways of a man all his iniquities will be atoned, so that he will look at the light of life, and in a Holy Spirit he will be united in his truth; and he will be cleansed from all his iniquities; and in an upright and humble spirit his sin will be atoned, and in the submission of his soul to the statutes of God his flesh will be cleansed, that he may be sprinkled with water for impurity and sanctify himself with water of cleanliness. And he will establish his steps, to walk perfectly in all the ways of God, as he commanded for the appointed times of his testimonies, and not to turn aside to right or left, and not to transgress against one of all his words. Then he will be accepted by pleasing atonements before God; and this will be for him a covenant of eternal community.*[4] The forerunner for Jesus was John the Baptist, who indeed echoed the thoughts of this early community. The Essenes, as a strict Jewish sect, lived in a manner which was reflected in John's appearance: *And the same John had his raiment of camel's hair, and a leathern girdle about his loins; and his meat was locusts and wild honey.* (Matthew 3:4) The Essenes lived in the desert, the Biblical equivalent of the wilderness (*In those days came John the Baptist, preaching in the wilderness of Judaea...* Matthew 3:1), they were forbidden from sacrificing animals (*...and his meat was locusts* *and wild honey...* Matthew 3:4), with most of their diet similar to vegetarianism, consisting mostly of roots, fruits, and bread. The truth about the Essenes is that they were largely rejected by the mainline Jewish communities, which desired political control via aggressive means, which the Essenes rejected, favoring peace and refusing to carry or use weapons. It appears the Essenes lived communally, and there were different orders of the group, some that married and some that didn't. John the Baptist's physical characteristics described to us do suggest that he was a member of the community before he began his evangelism, preparing the way for Jesus.

The relevancy of this is very far-reaching, and also very staggering. The realities of Judaism at the time of Jesus and just prior to Jesus are often very different than the picture we sometimes hear about. It was a politically tumultuous time, with Judaism already on its course to national and racial identity as a means to salvation rather than a relationship with God. As a result, Judaism was looking for a specific type of Messianic leader: one who would rush in and rescue them all from Roman occupation. With so much emphasis on politics, the spiritual components of the Messiah were pushed aside. That is where the Essenes come in: their dedication to remaining pure for God while awaiting the coming of the Messiah set forth spiritual focus rather than political aims. It was the perfect environment for John the Baptist to receive the training he needed to perform his work as the Messianic forerunner. Quotations from Essene works are found throughout the New Testament, from such notables as John the Baptist, Paul, and even Jesus Himself! Clearly this group had an impact on the spiritual perceptions of the Messiah, as the community as a group prepared the way by showing forth the connection between baptism and purification from sin, as could be seen in the quotation provided earlier. It is most appropriate that John would have belonged to a community that laid the foundations for the very ministry he went on to hold in the role of Christianity.

In Matthew 3 we interestingly enough note that John did not only baptize Jesus, but continued to baptize even after the baptism of Jesus in the Jordan. Although the Scriptures do not seem to suggest Jesus Himself baptized anyone in water, He Himself was baptized by John as a fulfillment of prophecy and both a symbol of the death and resurrection he would undergo for our sins. After the resurrection of Jesus, baptism continued to be a practice of the early church, usually one of if not the first experiences a new Christian had.

BAPTISM-LIKE TRADITIONS OUTSIDE OF CHRISTIANITY

But with the precious blood of Christ, as of a lamb without blemish and without spot: Who verily was foreordained before the foundation of the world, but was manifest in these last times for you, Who by Him do believe in God, that raised him up from the dead, and gave him glory; that your faith and hope might be in God.
- 1 Peter 1:19-21

Although it's not called baptism and not always a symbol of repentance, the notion that a water washing or immersion is a sign of starting over and becoming a part of something new stretches far beyond the limits of Christian understanding. Even though it doesn't mean the same thing, it is interesting to see that washing for the purpose of renewal is typed in various religious groups all over the world.

- **Sikhism** – All who are Sikhs are to be a part of the "Khalsa" ("pure") or aspiring to be such, which makes one fully united with the founder's teachings. Initiates receive a rite called baptism which involves the drinking of Amrit (sugar water mixed with a dagger) in the presence of five Sikhs who are already "khalsa" and the Guru Granth Sahib. The individual takes vows at this time to never remove hair from any part of the body, to refrain from alcohol, tobacco, and drug use, not eat meat slaughtered in the "Muslim" way, and to not commit adultery. Sikhs at this level are required to wear Sikh symbolism at all times and follow a Code of Conduct.

- **Gnosticism** – Gnostics, having combined Christian teachings with esoteric occultism, paganism, Judaism, Zoroastrianism, or eastern religion, was very diverse in its strains of teaching. However, the Mandean Gnostics held and hold repeated baptisms to this very day, symbolizing one's initiation into the Gnostic community and the beginning of rebirth in hidden knowledge. This group also shows evidence of a ceremony involving baptism for the dead.

- **Ancient Egypt** – Infant children were baptized, to purify them of imperfections possibly obtained while in utero.

- **Mormonism** – This religion has an elaborate initiation ceremony of baptism performed by drama and role-playing. Mormon baptism also employs a baptism of the dead, by which a member adopts the name of a deceased person and "stands in" for them in the ceremony, in the hopes that those who were unable to hear about Mormonism in this life might accept it in the next.

- **Judaism** – The ceremony of *mikvah* is the final stage to becoming a Jew. After classes and instruction, a converting Jew enters into a pool of water completely naked, goes under, and is believed to be "reborn" as a Jew.

- **Hinduism** – The Ganges River in India is believed to be the holiest river in the world, and that washing in it will remove one's sins.

<u>NON-BAPTIZING GROUPS</u>

How much more shall the blood of Christ, who through the eternal Spirit offered Himself without spot to God, purge your conscience from dead works to serve the living God?
Hebrews 9:14

In contrast to what we spoke of earlier, there are groups who have never believed baptism is relevant, from their start. Instead of following a modern trend that questions its symbolism, they have never embraced baptism or ritual washing or immersion as a part of their belief systems. Christian Science feels that everything must be spiritual, as there is a distinction between matter and spirit, and matter is evil. Therefore, Christian Scientists do not baptize in water. Unitarian Universalists do not baptize, but rather "welcome" infants into the community in a ceremony similar to a Wiccan naming ceremony, similar to a presentation in a Jewish temple. Catholics, although engaging in initiation ritual of baptism upon infants or new converts also believe in what is called "the baptism of blood," which teaches that martyrs who die for the church go to heaven whether or not they are water baptized because they have been baptized with their own blood. The Salvation Army, because it was originally started as a mission intending to send members to other churches, does not hold any sacraments, and does not perform baptisms. Quakers, believing in the inward light and the spiritualizing of everything also do not baptize. New Agers reject immersions or washing, although some occult counterparts do have initiation rites that are similar to baptismal concept. Buddhists and members of the Baha'i Faith also do not immerse or recognize baptism.

WHY IS BAPTISM IMPORTANT?

Know ye not, that so many of us as were baptized into Jesus Christ were baptized into His death? Therefore we are buried with Him by baptism into death: that like as Christ was raised up from the dead by the glory of the Father, even so we also should walk in newness of life.
- Romans 6:3-4

For as many of you as have been baptized into Christ have put on Christ.
- Galatians 3:27

Buried with Him in baptism, wherein also ye are risen with Him through the faith of the operation of God, Who hath raised Him from the dead.
- Colossians 2:12

And such were some of you: but ye are washed, but ye are sanctified, but ye are justified in the Name of the Lord Jesus, and by the Spirit of our God.
- 1 Corinthians 6:11

Baptism is important because through baptism, we are baptized into the death of Christ and risen to new life in Him (Romans 6:3-4). The Bible literally tells us that when we are baptized, we have put on Christ. It is a part of our sanctification and empowerment as believers, walking and receiving the new life promised to us in Christ this side of heaven.

A BAPTISMAL CANDIDATE...

But when they believed Philip preaching the things concerning the kingdom of God, and the Name of Jesus Christ, they were baptized, both men and women. Then Simon himself believed also: and when he was baptized, he continued with Philip, and wondered, beholding the miracles and signs which were done. Now when the apostles which were at Jerusalem heard that Samaria had received the word of God, they sent unto them Peter and John: Who, when they were come down, prayed for them, that they might receive the Holy Ghost: (For as yet He was fallen upon none of them: only they were baptized in the Name of the Lord Jesus).
- Acts 8:12-16

- In the Bible, we only see those society deemed to be adults receive the rite of baptism. In keeping with an understanding of ancient society, that means the individuals baptized were at least 12 to 14 years of age. The candidate must be at an age where they can have some understanding of sin and the consequences of sin in their lives. In short, they should have an understanding of right and wrong and be aware of wrongdoing. Some people call this the "age of reason." Most churches say this age happens somewhere around 7 and 10 years old. There are stories where individuals displayed this understanding as young as 4 and some who are not ready until they are significantly older. The age at which an individual truly displays their understanding of right and wrong can be different for everyone. Instead of looking at age, look at their level of understanding.

- A candidate must follow proper procedure for baptismal preparation, which we will discuss later.

- When preparing a baptismal candidate, the goal is not to see an individual who is perfect. If a baptismal candidate is a new believer, they most likely have many flaws and imperfections that will need ironing out over time. Don't use these issues against the individual to avoid baptism. Baptism is the beginning of new life in Christ, not the end. Performing baptism is most likely the thing they need to help set them even further on the road to a life of empowerment and holiness in Jesus Christ. The focus of baptism is believing in, understanding the life and redemptive work of, and trusting in Jesus Christ. It's the believer receiving and embracing Jesus – not the believer preparing for ordination or consecration.

WHAT IS NEEDED FOR BAPTISM?

Can any man forbid water, that these should not be baptized, which have received the Holy Ghost as well as we? And he commanded them to be baptized in the Name of the Lord. Then prayed they him to tarry certain days.
- Acts 10:47-48

Let us draw near with a true heart in full assurance of faith, having our hearts sprinkled from an evil conscience, and our bodies washed with pure water.
- Hebrews 10:22

In order to baptize, the following is needed:

- A water container sufficiently able to hold the minister and the candidate for baptism. The water level must be high enough for the individual to be completely submerged under water. This can be in the form of natural resources, such as a river, lake, or ocean. It can also be found in more modern sources, such as a pool, baptismal font, or a bathtub. The point is not so much whether you use a pool or a river, as do you have enough water to perform the baptism correctly.

- If a minister is not in a position to have access to natural sources or a baptismal font, local health clubs, spas, other ministries, or hotels all have access to pools or fonts. Inquire about using these facilities for baptism as needed.

- If someone is in danger of death and there is no water available, a prayer and the individual's faith will stand sufficient. A smaller amount of water can be used in such an emergency, but this is the exception rather than the rule.

CORRECT BAPTISMAL FORM

And as they went on their way, they came unto a certain water: and the eunuch said, See, here is water;
what doth hinder me to be baptized? And Philip said, If thou believest with all thine heart, thou mayest.
And he answered and said, I believe that Jesus Christ is the Son of God. And he commanded the chariot to stand still:
and they went down both into the water, both Philip and the eunuch; and he baptized him.
- Acts 8:36-38

The word "baptism" comes from the Greek word "baptizma" which literally means, "to bury," which directly expresses its symbolism. According to *Today's New International Version Bible Concordance*,[5] the word "baptize" means: *To wash, dip, or immerse in water. Baptism demonstrates death to self and an emergence as a new creation to live in Christ's Kingdom.*

Baptism is symbolic of burial. For this reason, the main element required to perform a valid baptism is plenty of water. Sprinkling as is done in many formal denominations is incorrect. Infant baptism is invalid as we can see repentance to be a decision one makes. As an infant is unable to make that decision, infant baptism is, therefore, invalid. Proxy baptisms are, likewise, invalid.

Baptisms are burials into the water – and rising out thereof. Baptismal form involves completely immersing the baptismal candidate into the water and then rising them out to new life.

WHO CAN BAPTIZE?

And it came to pass, that, while Apollos was at Corinth, Paul having passed through the upper coasts came to
Ephesus: and finding certain disciples, He said unto them, Have ye received the Holy Ghost since ye believed?
And they said unto him, We have not so much as heard whether there be any Holy Ghost. And he said unto them,
Unto what then were ye baptized? And they said, Unto John's baptism. Then said Paul, John verily baptized with
the baptism of repentance, saying unto the people, that they should believe on him which should come after him,
that is, on Christ Jesus. When they heard this, they were baptized in the Name of the Lord Jesus.
- Acts 19:1-5

In the Bible, we see baptism done by leaders:

- John the Baptist, who was a prophet and type of an apostle.

- The apostles themselves, on the day of Pentecost and throughout the book of Acts.

- Philip, an Evangelist, baptizes the eunuch.

- The Apostle Paul speaks of baptizing individuals in the Corinthian church.

- Other leaders are spoken of as having baptized individuals in the Corinthian church. We are unsure of their position within the church, but as we understand the system by which they appear to have been employing baptism, they were clearly leaders of some sort.

- Every admonition to baptism was conveyed through leadership.

In following with God's established order, the baptismal rite should, therefore, be performed by a leader. Within the jurisdiction of the United States and several countries worldwide, a leader performing a baptism must be validly licensed and ordained.

BAPTISMAL FORMULA

Go ye therefore, and teach all nations, baptizing them in the Name of the Father, and of the Son, and of the Holy Ghost.
— Matthew 28:19

Then said Paul, John verily baptized with the baptism of repentance, saying unto the people, that they should believe on Him which should come after him, that is, on Christ Jesus. When they heard this, they were baptized in the Name of the Lord Jesus.
- Acts 19:4-5

Now when they heard this, they were pricked in their heart, and said unto Peter and to the rest of the apostles, Men and brethren, what shall we do? Then Peter said unto them, Repent, and be baptized every one of you in the Name of Jesus Christ for the remission of sins, and ye shall receive the gift of the Holy Ghost.
— Acts 2:38

Debates abound about the correct formula to use for baptism. Some people modify the Word and use their own formula. Some groups embrace Matthew 28:19; others embrace Acts 2:38 or other verses found within the New Testament. Some groups use a combination of both.

The purpose of this book is not to argue over whether Matthew 28:19 or Acts 2:38 should be used for baptismal purposes. Over the past several years, especially since the first printing of this book, I have given much consideration to the debates and even re-examined my own position on it. If we look at the book of Acts and the experiences of the early apostles, they baptized in the Name of Jesus Christ. We can understand this in the light of Matthew 28:19. To say that within the Name of Christ is the Name of the Father and the Son (as Jesus means "Jehovah saves") and that the Holy Spirit comes in His Name, we see there is powerful truth that within the Name of Jesus, we find the Father, the Son, and the Holy Spirit. At the same time, I don't believe that Matthew 28:19 was ever intended to be cryptic. The Bible itself teaches us there is only one baptism, and that must mean that we can incorporate both Matthew 28:19 and Acts 2:38 into our baptismal formula. Baptism should expand beyond the bounds of a singular verse, including examples and methods found throughout the New Testament. Baptism is an experience, not just a formula. We spend so much time fixated on what we say before we immerse the individual that we forget about the numerous stories and examples of baptism found throughout the New Testament.

I don't believe it is the Christian way to create such conflict over what we say in baptism. I also believe that we can't deny the Scriptures instruct us to do all that we do in the Name of Jesus Christ: we have life through His Name (John 20:31), we are healed (Mark 6:22-23, Acts 3:6, 4:10, 4:30), preach boldly (Acts 9:27, 9:29), we are justified (1 Corinthians 6:11), we give thanks (Ephesians 5:20), withdraw ourselves from those who do not walk in truth (2 Thessalonians 3:6), request and pray (John 14:13-14, 15:16, 16:23-26), believe (1 John 3:23), and most of all, do all (Colossians 3:17). We can't take Jesus out of baptism! This tells me one thing: the way we should handle baptism is to speak both Matthew 28:19 and Acts 2:38 when we perform baptismal rites. This method is a long-standing tradition in many Baptist, Church of Christ, and Pentecostal churches, and it is a way that ends controversy, strife, and upholds baptism for what it is rather than making it a right-fight.

As the individual is placed under the water, the following should be said:

"(Insert recipient's name), I baptize you, in the Name of the Father, and of the Son, and of the Holy Spirit – in the Name of Jesus Christ for the remission of sins, and ye shall receive the gift of the Holy Ghost."

The individual should then be brought up again out of the water.

MINISTER PRESENTATION

Which sometime were disobedient, when once the longsuffering of God waited in the days of Noah, while the ark was a preparing, wherein few, that is, eight souls were saved by water. The like figure whereunto even baptism doth also now save us (not the putting away of the filth of the flesh, but the answer of a good conscience toward God,) by the resurrection of Jesus Christ: Who is gone into heaven, and is on the right hand of God; angels and authorities and powers being made subject unto Him.
– I Peter 3:20-22

Ministers should align themselves accordingly for baptism. Baptism is not a trip to the beach or the pool, but a spiritual experience. That means a minister performing a baptism must look the part, present as the part, and take into consideration the people present to receive and witness a baptism.

Baptism is a different experience for a minister, especially when a minister is used to pulpit ministry. If a minister thinks ministry is all about expensive suits or robes, they must reassess their concepts to officiate at a baptism. Baptism isn't an occasion for a three-piece suit. It is, likewise, not an occasion for an expensive robe or mantle. Baptism is a relatively informal ceremony, involving water and nature, simple and to-the-point. It is not long and drawn out. As a rule, it is also not a time for extensive preaching and teaching. The rite of baptism speaks for itself, and stands as an important bridge between the church and the believer. As a result, it is also a powerful witness for both saved and unsaved alike who may be present for the rite.

The minister of God should present themselves simply for a baptism.

Many public pools will not allow people in the pool in their street clothes which requires the minister to make an investment for baptismal purposes. A bathing suit should be worn underneath a white garment specifically used for baptismal purposes. The outer garment serves both modesty purposes and ritual purposes: it establishes the ceremony as more than just a poolside party. Some companies sell relatively inexpensive robes that are mildew-proof and washable for baptismal purposes. A basic robe, a tunic-like robe or long shirt, or some other garment should be worn for the baptism. As baptisms involve water, the minister runs the risk of going under water, getting wet, or getting smudged. It is not a ceremony that should involve make-up, expensive hair styles, or jewelry. Outer baptismal garments should be fluid and not excessively form-fitting, and should not be easily caught or damaged.

Towels should be available to dry off after baptism and an alternate change of clothes should be available, if necessary. Clothing for the event should remain appropriate, neat, and casual.

Ministers should read the Word, express interest in the event, and talk to guests and members present. A minister of God should never be hidden in a back room, waiting to descend upon the people. Baptism is a celebration: the individual who is baptized is dying to their flesh and rising in the Spirit. Ministers should not shy away from questions and make sure that the purpose of baptism is clear to those present, in case there are questions.

BAPTISMAL PREPARATION

But when the kindness and love of God our Savior appeared, He saved us, not because of righteous things we had done, but because of His mercy. He saved us through the washing of rebirth and renewal by the Holy Spirit, Whom He poured out on us generously through Jesus Christ our Savior, so that, having been justified by His grace, we might become heirs having the hope of eternal life.
- Titus 3:4-7 (NIV)

If a person is serious about baptism, they will prepare for baptism. Most churches and ministries have a program available for baptismal preparation. When preparing a baptismal preparation program, keep in mind a few basic things. The first is that baptism is something typically done quickly, if not immediately, after repentance and conversion. A baptism class shouldn't be something long and drawn out for weeks and months at a time. The basic things to look for when someone seeks baptism is their understanding of Christ's atonement for their sins, a heart of repentance, and a true desire to transform into the person Christ desires them to become. This doesn't require extensive doctrinal training; that comes about through years of study and involvement with the Body of Christ. Just as the Evangelist Philip witnessed to the eunuch, expounding the Word to him, and then baptized him immediately, we should too recognize this to be a solid system for baptism. A basic understanding of Christ should be provided – and demonstrated – and baptism made available.

The baptism recipient should be made aware of the importance in appropriateness and modesty in appearance. Bathing suits for women should be one-piece or covered with a shirt or cover-all. Male recipients should wear an appropriately fitting shorts/trunks swimsuit, not exceedingly tight, with a white T-shirt. They should be advised to bring a change of clothes and instructed in the casual nature of the baptismal rite. Both men and women should be advised against wearing make-up and jewelry. The baptismal recipient may also want to invite others, and should be told this is acceptable during the preparation process. This is an appropriate situation for both believers and non-believers to attend as a witness to the faith.

Because the baptism itself is central, discuss with the recipient if they would like any sort of special element, such as a special song, prayer, words, or reading. Incorporate any of these elements into the ceremony, as these will make it unique and special to the individual and the work of God within them.

Some churches combine baptism and membership classes, and desire to see the candidate show a certain aptitude of all things Christian in order to be baptized. Baptism should never be used as a bait for church or ministry membership. In baptism, one is baptized into Christ – not into a denomination. If a baptism is being used as a leverage to try and mandate one join a religious group or church, baptism is not following according to Biblical formula: that of being baptized into Christ.

When one is operating a Biblical ministry, they will offer baptism as an option to all the members and will readily baptize those who are interested as often as the issue arises.

CEREMONY

A baptismal ceremony should be relatively simple. The focus of the ceremony is the baptism itself, the going down into the water and the rising up again.

The baptismal ceremony itself should begin next to the water used for the baptism. The minister should introduce the rite, explaining a little bit about it, introducing the baptismal candidate and allowing them to speak a little on their choice of baptism, if they so desire. If a special selection is to be or read, it can be read now.

Both the minister and recipient go into the water and prepare for the rite.

The minister states the baptismal formula as the individual goes under the water:

" (Insert recipient's name), I baptize you, in the Name of the Father, and of the Son, and of the Holy Spirit – in the Name of Jesus Christ for the remission of sins, and ye shall receive the gift of the Holy Ghost."

Candidate is completely submerged and brought back up again.

Ceremony may follow with any other special elements, such as a special prayer or song.

Once candidate and minister are dry, present a certificate of baptism to the candidate.

BAPTISM DOS AND DON'TS:

- DO embrace baptism and the relevance of it for believers.
- DO study the history of baptism and learn more of why it is important.
- DO learn the different viewpoints and types that exist as pertain to baptism.

- DO teach on the importance of baptism.
- DO see baptism as a part of the Gospel message.
- DO prepare candidates for baptism.
- DO baptize by full immersion.
- DO baptize as the apostles did: in Jesus' Name, for the forgiveness of sins.
- DO answer questions, speak to guests, and interact with those present during the baptism ceremony.
- DO meet with a baptismal candidate prior to the baptism to discuss the ceremony and the significance of the ordinance, and the importance of modest presentation during baptism.
- DO invest in a cover-all or baptismal robe for baptism.
- DO incorporate special elements, such as Scripture readings or music, into the baptismal ceremony.
- DO present the baptismal recipient with a Certificate of Baptism.

- DON'T baptize infants or children who have not yet reached an age of reason.
- DON'T "sprinkle" in baptism.
- DON'T alter Biblical form, language, or wording in baptism.
- DON'T treat baptism as a bait for church membership.
- DON'T expect candidates for baptism to behave perfectly, modeling the perfect example of the Christian life.
- DON'T prohibit family, friends, and non-believers from attending a baptism.
- DON'T overdress for the occasion.

COMMUNION ELEMENTS

CHAPTER TEN

Communion

The cup of blessing which we bless, is it not the communion of the blood of Christ? The bread which we break, is it not the communion of the body of Christ?
- 1 Corinthians 10:16

WHAT IS COMMUNION?

Now He that ministereth seed to the sower both minister bread for your food, and multiply your seed sown, and increase the fruits of your righteousness; Being enriched in every thing to all bountifulness, which causeth through us thanksgiving to God.
-2 Corinthians 9:10-11

The term "communion" is used to refer to two main things. The first is the unity of individuals, God, or both, and their interaction as a result of their unity. Within that unity there is both spiritual and practical understanding. The second is the memorial of the Lord's death, often called "the last supper." It is impossible to divide these two understandings as we explore the deeper meanings and sacred purpose behind communion, celebrating communion, and walking in the Lord's decency and order as we memorialize Jesus' death until He comes again.

WHY IS COMMUNION IMPORTANT?

There is one body, and one Spirit, even as ye are called in one hope of your calling...One God and Father of all,

Who is above all, and through all, and in you all.
- Ephesians 4:4,6

The current understanding of communion tends to be limited to the monthly, quarterly, "fifth Sunday" or yearly communion service performed in a local church. This limitation exists because the modern church has no understanding of unity. The foundation of unity is found first in understanding the church is bigger than a local church of believers. The church is the Body of Christ, made up of believers found in every country worldwide. We are united because we are all in Christ, and we are united in Christ because of His atoning work. The promise of Galatians 3:27-29: *"For as many of you as have been baptized into Christ have put on Christ. There is neither Jew nor Greek, there is neither bond nor free, there is neither male nor female: for ye are all one in Christ Jesus. And if ye be Christ's, then are ye Abraham's seed, and heirs according to the promise."* begins with our unity in Christ. If we are not striving to be one with our Lord and one another, we are not going to understand the power present in communion.

Every minister should strive to understand the importance of unity. When the leaders of God understand communion as an extension of unity (both with God and one another), it changes the way communion is viewed, embraced, and presented. Divisions in the church are due to the misunderstandings of human beings: their misinterpretations, their misrepresentations, and their own disagreements. We see division when we are unable to come together and reason. Communion brings us back into a place where the church has the power and potential to be one. In communion is the grace for healing, power, and true reconciliation with God and among the saints.

IS COMMUNION JUST ABOUT A CHURCH SERVICE DONE A FEW TIMES PER YEAR?

The grace of the Lord Jesus Christ, and the love of God, and the communion of the Holy Ghost,
be with you all. Amen.
- 2 Corinthians 13:14

It's easy to think communion is just about the service. The majority of churches do not talk about communion on the weeks they do not hold the physical communion service. Even though we drop the words "unity" and "fellowship" around quite frequently, it's unusual to hear teaching that expands the individual beyond their own immediate relationship with God and into the Kingdom of God.

Our relationship with God is not just about God and us; it's also about each one of us and our relationship to others in the Body of Christ. Unity begins in our communion and fellowship with God, and then moves to our interactions with one another. Communion is an expression of this unity and a reminder of the call to be one.

Communion is not just about a service, or about the elements themselves. Communion is a call, a reminder, an expression, and a purpose. In the breaking of the bread, we remember our own call to "break," to reach a point where God can work within us and we can work with others, to reach the point of spiritual breakthrough. In the cup, we see the need to pour out ourselves, emptying ourselves so we can be filled with Him. We are a part of His Body; a unity, a part of one another, and a part of something that requires us to dig deeper than our surface selves. If we embrace the rite of communion, it is about our relationship with God, the expression of the Holy Spirit in our lives, the transforming work of the Spirit within us, unity with our leaders, and unity one to another with every believer worldwide. It's about those we know, those we don't know, and those we will never know until we arrive in heaven or Jesus returns.

HOW OFTEN SHOULD WE HOLD COMMUNION?

For as often as ye eat this bread, and drink this cup, ye do shew the Lord's death till He come.
— I Corinthians 11:26

Different denominations have adopted different practices pertaining to communion. In some churches, communion is done once per month, on a Sunday selected by the leadership. In other churches, communion is done quarterly, or once every three months. Still, in others, communion is done once per year, or less. There are a few denominations that observe the rite of communion every week. There are even denominations that reject communion all together, and never hold a physical communion service.

The variances within the frequency of communion practices exist because the New Testament does not give us a specified requirement as to how many times per year the church should observe communion. What we see instead is attentive detail to how communion is observed and the relevance of form and teaching associated with it. This tells us two things:

- It is more relevant how we observe communion in form than in frequency.

- We should be open to celebrating communion in remembrance of the Lord as often as the opportunity arises.

WHERE SHOULD WE HOLD COMMUNION?

Now the first day of the Feast of Unleavened Bread the disciples came to Jesus, saying unto Him,
Where wilt Thou that we prepare for Thee to eat the Passover? And He said, Go into the city to such a man,
and say unto him, The Master saith, My time is at hand; I will keep the Passover at thy house with My disciples.
And the disciples did as Jesus had appointed them; and they made ready the Passover. Now when the even was come,
He sat down with the twelve.
— Matthew 26:17-20

And when He had given thanks, He brake it, and said, Take, eat: this is My body, which is broken for you:
this do in remembrance of Me.
— 1 Corinthians 11:24

Communion services are often limited to the local church during a weekly service. We have no specification that communion can only be held in church. Communion services should be held as a part of a Sunday service, however many times per year as directed. This celebrates the unity of the church and reminds all about the unity that should be found therein.

These aren't the only occasions for communion, however. Communion services should be present at any type of event that unite believers with God and with one another. These can include:

- Special-themed conferences (women, men, youth, etc.)
- Leadership conferences and events
- Weddings

- Ordinations
- Funerals
- Church dinners/occasions
- Friendship gatherings
- Other events signifying unity

WHO RECEIVES COMMUNION?

Wherefore whosoever shall eat this bread, and drink this cup of the Lord, unworthily, shall be guilty of the body and blood of the Lord. But let a man examine himself, and so let him eat of that bread, and drink of that cup. For he that eateth and drinketh unworthily, eateth and drinketh damnation to himself, not discerning the Lord's body. For this cause many are weak and sickly among you, and many sleep. For if we would judge ourselves, we should not be judged. But when we are judged, we are chastened of the Lord, that we should not be condemned with the world. Wherefore, my brethren, when ye come together to eat, tarry one for another. And if any man hunger, let him eat at home; that ye come not together unto condemnation. And the rest will I set in order when I come.
- 1 Corinthians 11:27-34

Some denominations have requirements about who can receive communion. These requirements pertain to age appropriate reception of communion, church membership, or being a Christian. Other denominations may not have any requirements or may be very lax in their position about receiving communion.

Communion is about unity, which means it is wrong to take a position against communion guidelines. By taking communion, one is not just stating unity with the Lord, but also with the Body of Christ. When Jesus passed around the communion elements at the Last Supper, each individual was given the freedom to choose to partake, and even He did not interfere with who should or should not take communion. This means that discerning about communion and taking the elements should be based on personal discernment and discretion. No one should receive the communion elements if they are uncertain about their relationship with the Lord or about being a Christian. That having been said, the requirements to receive communion are as follows:

- Must be a believer in the Lord Jesus Christ as Savior, recognizing and receiving His atonement on the cross for their sins.

- Must believe in the Body of Christ, the church, and the relevance of being connected to that larger body.

- Must believe in the conditions of unity, the "fundamentals of faith," laid out in Ephesians 4:1-32.

- Children should not be prohibited from receiving, but at the same time, should understand what is going on and should conduct themselves with reverence when receiving communion. Whether or not to allow a child to participate in communion is at the jurisdiction of their parents or guardians.

WHAT IS NEEDED FOR COMMUNION?

And as they were eating, Jesus took bread, and blessed it, and brake it, and gave it to the disciples, and said, Take, eat; this is My body. And He took the cup, and gave thanks, and gave it to them, saying, Drink ye all of it; For this is My blood of the new testament, which is shed for many for the remission of sins. But I say unto you, I will not drink henceforth of this fruit of the vine, until that day when I drink it new with you in my Father's kingdom. And when they had sung an hymn, they went out into the mount of Olives.
- Matthew 26:26-30

In order to hold a communion service, the following is needed:

- Unleavened bread in some form (wafers, homemade, purchased, etc.).

- The fruit of the vine, a reference to a grape juice or wine.

- A communion set suitable for the occasion, which should consist of:

  - A bread tray, plate or paten for the distribution of unleavened bread.
  - A Single-Pass/Whole Body Communion tray for distribution of grape juice or wine.
  - Small, disposable plastic or paper cups for the distribution of grape juice or wine or a chalice from which the assembly all

drink from in communion (and a cloth or napkins to wipe the chalice).

- Music, that the people of God may sing the praises of God.

- Some churches also have a communion table or altar in the front of the church for the distribution of the elements.

COMMUNION ELEMENTS

I am that bread of life. Your fathers did eat manna in the wilderness, and are dead. This is the bread which cometh down from heaven, that a man may eat thereof, and not die. I am the living bread which came down from heaven: if any man eat of this bread, he shall live for ever: and the bread that I will give is my flesh, which I will give for the life of the world. The Jews therefore strove among themselves, saying, How can this man give us his flesh to eat? Then Jesus said unto them, Verily, verily, I say unto you, Except ye eat the flesh of the Son of man, and drink his blood, ye have no life in you. Whoso eateth My flesh, and drinketh My blood, hath eternal life; and I will raise him up at the last day. For my flesh is meat indeed, and my blood is drink indeed. He that eateth my flesh, and drinketh my blood, dwelleth in me, and I in him. As the living Father hath sent me, and I live by the Father: so he that eateth Me, even he shall live by Me. This is that bread which came down from heaven: not as your fathers did eat manna, and are dead: he that eateth of this bread shall live for ever.
- John 6:48-58

Therefore let us keep the feast, not with old leaven, neither with the leaven of malice and wickedness; but with the unleavened bread of sincerity and truth.
- 1 Corinthians 5:8

When ye come together therefore into one place, this is not to eat the Lord's supper. For in eating every one taketh before other his own supper: and one is hungry, and another is drunken. What? have ye not houses to eat and to drink in? or despise ye the church of God, and shame them that have not? what shall I say to you? shall I praise you in this? I praise you not. For I have received of the Lord that which also I delivered unto you, that the Lord Jesus the same night in which He was betrayed took bread: And when He had given thanks, He brake it, and said, Take, eat: this is My body, which is broken for you: this do in remembrance of Me. After the same manner also He took the cup, when He had supped, saying, this cup is the new testament in My blood: this do ye, as oft as ye drink it, in remembrance of Me.
- 1 Corinthians 11:20-25

Communion is a memorial of the Lord's death. It reminds us of His sacrifice on the cross for our sins, that we might live in His redemption. It signifies grace, love, sacrifice, and the resurrection. It also is a reminder of unity, as we spoke of earlier: communion with God and with one another.

It is important that we do not treat communion elements lightly. As they represent the Body and Blood of Christ, we cannot feel the right to use any sort of item we so please. Many churches use whatever they have most ready to them without any forethought to the significance therein.

The first communion service took place on the night before Jesus Christ was crucified, on the first night of Passover. As part of the Passover meal, Jews to this day eat unleavened bread and drink wine or grape juice. Both items were a part of the Passover memorial, recalling when the people of God left Egypt (Exodus 12:1-51). They are highly significant in their purpose, and we cannot think to substitute them with other items.

Leavening is used throughout the Bible to represent sin (Exodus 23:18, Leviticus 2:11, Matthew 16:6-12, Mark 8:14-15, Luke 12:1-2,1 Corinthians 5:5-8, Galatians 5:9). Unleavened bread represents the sinless life of Christ and His atonement to make sinners the sons and daughters of God (Matthew 26:26, 1 Corinthians 11:24). It also extends, as Christ is saying the unleavened bread is His Body, to the church, the Bride of Christ, called to be without stain, spot, or wrinkle (Ephesians 5:27). When preparing communion, unleavened bread or a form of unleavened bread must be employed.

The "fruit of the vine" is used to represent blood (Genesis 49:11, Mark 14:24). This is an obvious reference to Jesus' blood, shed for the sins of many. It was a passing from the sacrificial system, completed in Christ, to the operation of grace. Communion reminds us of the saving power of the blood of Jesus and its importance in our own sanctification and the sanctification of the church. It also represents Christ as the vine and we as the branches (John 15:1-5), once again, signifying our union with Him and one another. When preparing communion, it is customary to use grape juice as opposed to wine. The only difference between the two is wine contains alcohol and fermentation and grape juice contains neither. Both are from the vine, made from grapes, with the same symbolism and representation. Because the fruit of the vine represents blood, there is no requirement to use fermented wine in the ceremonial process. In fact, using grape juice echoes to the process of God, the natural process and creation of the Lord, without the use or assistance of man in its creation. As we can see in Isaiah 65:8, it is our place to advocate the integrity of the Lord's cup through grape juice: *As the new wine is found in the cluster, And one says, "Do not destroy it, For a blessing is in it," So will I do for My servants' sake, That I may not destroy them all.* This also allows for all people to partake of communion – children, adults, substance abusers, alcoholics, and advocates of temperance.

It is also worth noting that communion is not a snack time for the church. Communion should be distributed appropriately and partaken appropriately. It is inappropriate for any church member to take more than one piece of unleavened bread and one small cup or sip of grape juice.

WHO CAN ADMINISTER COMMUNION?

And they told what things were done in the way, and how He was known of them in breaking of bread.
- Luke 24:35

Following after Jesus, Who distributed communion to His first followers, the recitation, blessing, and declarations during communion should be done by a leader. The leader administering communion can be any leader found within the five-fold (apostle, prophet, evangelist, pastor, or teacher).

In following with God's established order, the communion rite should be administered by a validly ordained and licensed minister. This also reflects remaining in order with the laws established by our government.

Communion should be distributed by those involved in ministries of help and assistance, such as bishops, deacons and elders.

COMMUNION FORMULA

And as they did eat, Jesus took bread, and blessed, and brake it, and gave to them, and said, Take, eat:
this is My body. And He took the cup, and when He had given thanks, He gave it to them: and they all drank of it.
And He said unto them, This is My blood of the new testament, which is shed for many. Verily I say unto you,
I will drink no more of the fruit of the vine, until that day that I drink it new in the Kingdom of God.
And when they had sung an hymn, they went out into the mount of Olives.
- Mark 14:22-26

For I have received of the Lord that which also I delivered unto you, that the Lord Jesus the same night in which

He was betrayed took bread: And when He had given thanks, he brake it, and said, Take, eat: this is My body, which is broken for you: this do in remembrance of Me. After the same manner also He took the cup, when He had supped, saying, this cup is the new testament in My blood: this do ye, as oft as ye drink it, in remembrance of Me. For as often as ye eat this bread, and drink this cup, ye do shew the Lord's death till He come.
- I Corinthians 11:23-26

Most churches follow a similar format for communion that holds to Biblical pattern. A short word is delivered on communion, there is the reading of the Scriptural passage on the Last Supper, communion is distributed, and the words of Jesus pertaining to communion elements is read before the church or assembly present partakes of the elements.

Those present should be advised of the nature of communion and its importance. They should be given a few moments of reflectivity for pause, to assess themselves and whether or not they should partake. The guidelines for partaking should be clarified at this time.

A Bible passage reflecting communion should be read, and then the communion elements distributed. Communion is typically distributed one of three ways:

- To the congregation directly, in their seats, via trays, passed to everyone.

- Requiring the congregation to come to the front of the church to receive the elements themselves.

- Requiring the congregation to come to the front of the church, distributing the elements to the congregation one person at a time.

Communion elements should be prayed over and communion itself should include prayer for reception, thanksgiving, and blessing.

The following words are stated during communion either a) before people come forward to receive of elements at the altar (in that instance, the two phrases are spoken together), or b) when the communion elements are received by everyone, and they have returned to their seats, ready to partake:

"And as they were eating, Jesus took bread, and blessed it, and brake it, and gave it to the disciples, and said, Take, eat; this is My body."

Everyone then partakes of the bread of communion.

"And He took the cup, and gave thanks, and gave it to them, saying, Drink ye all of it; For this is my blood of the new testament, which is shed for many for the remission of sins."

Everyone then partakes of the fruit of the vine of communion.

Communion should conclude with music of some sort, giving individuals time to reflect and to praise God.

FOOT-WASHING SERVICE AND COMMUNION

Now before the feast of the Passover, when Jesus knew that His hour was come that he should depart out of this world unto the Father, having loved His own which were in the world, he loved them unto the end.
And supper being ended, the devil having now put into the heart of Judas Iscariot, Simon's son, to betray Him;
Jesus knowing that the Father had given all things into His hands, and that He was come from God,
and went to God; He riseth from supper, and laid aside His garments; and took a towel, and girded Himself.
After that He poureth water into a bason, and began to wash the disciples' feet, and to wipe them with the towel wherewith He was girded. Then cometh He to Simon Peter: and Peter saith unto Him, Lord, dost Thou wash my feet?
Jesus answered and said unto Him, What I do thou knowest not now; but thou shalt know hereafter.
Peter saith unto Him, Thou shalt never wash my feet. Jesus answered him, If I wash thee not, thou hast no part with Me. Simon Peter saith unto him, Lord, not my feet only, but also my hands and my head. Jesus saith to him, He that is washed needeth not save to wash his feet, but is clean every whit: and ye are clean, but not all.
For He knew who should betray Him; therefore said He, Ye are not all clean. So after He had washed their feet, and had taken His garments, and was set down again, He said unto them, Know ye what I have done to you?
Ye call me Master and Lord: and ye say well; for so I am. If I then, your Lord and Master, have washed your feet; ye also ought to wash one another's feet. For I have given you an example, that ye should do as I have done to you. Verily, verily, I say unto you, The servant is not greater than his lord; neither he that is sent greater than he that sent him. If ye know these things, happy are ye if ye do them.
- John 13:1-17

Many churches observe a foot-washing service as part of communion. As in accordance with Christ's command to wash one another's feet, this calls to mind our unity in the Body through service to one another.

Foot-washing was done as part of ancient custom. As people did not have shoes or sneakers in those days (if they had anything at all, they had sandals), their feet were easily dirtied by sand and dirt. To this day, people in the Middle East eat on the floor, reclining on pillows, with their hands. It is obvious why it was so important feet were clean: tracking in dirt or sand could contaminate food or contaminate the household. Washing feet was the job of one of the household servants and considered the lowest of low jobs, the ultimate symbol of servant-hood.

It's not an accident Jesus instructed His followers to be servants. It is also not an accident that these words were spoken to people who would become foundational leaders within the early church. Foot-washing is a powerful reminder for leaders to remember:

- Their call to ministry is one of a servant, not one of a slave-driver. While those who study or train under a leader may desire to be of servant to that leader, the purpose in ministry is not to be served, but to serve.

- Ministry serves with humility, not with pride. Successful ministers are humble, not proud or haughty.

- Ministers are called to take up their cross and follow Christ, even in the midst of those who will betray them, because inevitably, leaders will encounter betrayal.

- Ministry is about more than just preaching or pulpit work; it is about being involved and "down and dirty," so to speak, in making the Gospel real to those God sends us to serve.

For those not in church leadership, foot-washing is a powerful reminder:

- Servant-hood is not just about a leader's call. As we are called to submit to one another (Ephesians 5:21), we are also called to serve one another. It is not just the leader's job to be of service; it is everybody's job to be of service.

- Being a servant is action, not just words. Loving our neighbor is an action, not just words.

- No competition should exist in the church. Human beings can be proud and competitive by nature, but competition has no place in the life of a believer. Washing one another's feet provides an important leveling ground among believers, reminding them that no matter what they do or who they may be in the world, in the church they are gifted for service.

The way foot-washing is done varies among groups. Some only have the leaders wash feet of members, while others have members wash one another's feet. Because foot-washing is a reminder of service, all members should participate in foot-washing, washing one another's feet. As a guideline for comfort and boundaries, men should wash the feet of men and women should find the feet of women.

To perform a foot-washing ritual, the following is needed:

- A basin of water for each pair or group of people participating in the ritual.

- A towel for each pair or group of people participating in the ritual.

- Women participating should be advised against wearing full pantyhose (knee-highs are fine) and from wearing short skirts that could cause the person washing their feet to feel uncomfortable due to immodesty. Men should keep the same in mind, wearing appropriate-fitting pants.

Foot-washing should be done after the communion service. The scripture, John 13:1-17, should be read and then the congregation or assembly instructed to do likewise.

For various reasons, the foot-washing ritual may not be done during every communion service. The ability to provide the needed items, time factors, and other circumstances may prohibit a foot-washing ritual. Communion is still valid, and can still be performed, even if foot-washing cannot be done.

MINISTER PRESENTATION

Be ye followers of me, even as I also am of Christ. Now I praise you, brethren, that ye remember me in all things, and keep the ordinances, as I delivered them to you.
- I Corinthians 11:1-2

Communion should be treated as a special occasion. People of every culture wear their finest clothing for holidays, and communion should reflect the presentation we desire to give a holiday. Everyone involved in the communion participation should align accordingly, from the officiating minister to those who distribute communion elements.

Communion is a formal ceremony, involving the elements of bread, wine, and the community at large. It is an appropriate occasion for formal suits and dresses, and the formal wear of a minister. Ministers should never stand up to offer communion in a sloppy manner, poorly or improperly dressed.

If communion is offered as part of an informal event (such as a youth meeting or conference), leaders can dress casually, but must still maintain the integrity of neatness, cleanness, and appropriate attire.

COMMUNION PREPARATION

...And the rest will I set in order when I come.
- I Corinthians 11:34

Most churches do not offer any sort of formal preparation in the reception or formality of distributing communion. This leaves communion distributors and recipients to draw their own conclusions about communion distribution and reception.

Communion supplies (cups, trays, wafers if used, grape juice, etc.) should be on hand for every ministry, in the event of their need. If the church is also planning a foot-washing ritual, the supplies for foot-washing should also be on hand (basins, towels, and water). Supplies should be checked and stocked in anticipation of an upcoming communion event. If homemade bread is to be used, an appropriate recipe should be found and it should be prepared in the appropriate quantity for the appropriate service.

Deacons, elders, and other church leaders selected to work in the distribution of communion should be instructed in protocol. Distribution of communion will depend upon the church, its needs, its size, and the availability of materials to distribute communion. Those who will perform this important function should receive education in the following:

- Preparation of communion elements.
- Attitude and conduct for a minister of communion during the communion service.
- How communion will be distributed.
- The specific plan for communion distribution.
- The specific duties of each person involved in the process.
- Dress code for communion administration.
- Clean-up duties post communion.
- Preparation and distribution of foot-washing items (seeing basins have water and towels).
- Distribution of foot-washing items.

It's uncommon to find communion preparation classes. If a leader approaches the rite as a whole, formal preparation to receive communion is unnecessary. What a leader should do is make the important and essential themes of communion an integrated part of church understanding. This means that the leader of a church should either teach on or offer classes on unity and fellowship in order to understand the symbolism present there.

Before communion is distributed, the leader should talk a little bit about communion. Some use the entire service to devote to teaching about communion; others just seek to set the communion rite within another service. Either way, people should be informed of the protocol: how communion will be received, and by whom. Those present should be reminded to perform a personal examination of conscience, and to receive communion worthily, instead of unworthily.

CEREMONY

The basic communion ceremony is simple, as it is usually done as a service within a service or event. The focus of communion is on Christ, the unity present in Christ, and that unity symbolized in the elements of unleavened bread and grape juice. The altar of the church or communion table may use special decoration, such as a cloth or flowers, to commemorate the occasion. The communion elements should be present for all to see and pre-prepared for reception.

Communion service should start wherever the ceremony is to take place: a sanctuary, site for a church meal, a wedding, etc. The minister should introduce the rite, speaking a little bit about communion, and about the importance of receiving communion worthily. This is followed by the Scripture reading pertaining to communion. Suggested passages include:

- Matthew 26:17-30
- Mark 14:12-26
- Luke 22:7-20
- John 6:26-58
- Acts 2:42-47
- I Corinthians 10:16-17
- I Corinthians 11:18-34

After the reading of the Word, a prayer of thanksgiving, unity, and fellowship over the communion elements should follow.

Protocol then follows for the distribution of communion to the entire congregation:

- Communion is distributed to everyone in their seats, or –

- All come forward to receive the communion elements and bring them back to their seats.

Once all receive communion elements and are in their respective places, the minister states the following:

And as they were eating, Jesus took bread, and blessed it, and brake it, and gave it to the disciples, and said, Take, eat; this is My body. Take and eat.

Congregation then partakes of the bread of communion.
Once finished with the bread, the leader states the following:

And He took the cup, and gave thanks, and gave it to them, saying, Drink ye all of it; For this is my blood of the new testament, which is shed for many for the remission of sins. But I say unto you, I will not drink henceforth of this fruit of the vine, until that day when I drink it new with you in my Father's kingdom. Drink ye all of it.

Communion should end with a song of praise or a time of worship, all of which are invited to join in. It can be pre-recorded, or live.

Protocol follows for the distribution of communion at the altar:
Before recipients come to the altar to partake of communion, the minister states the following:

For I have received of the Lord that which also I delivered unto you, that the Lord Jesus the same night in which He was betrayed took bread: And when He had given thanks, He brake it, and said, Take, eat: this is My body, which is broken for you: this do in remembrance of Me. After the same manner also He took the cup, when He had supped, saying, this cup is the new testament in my blood: this do ye, as oft as ye drink it, in remembrance of Me. For as often as ye eat this bread, and drink this cup, ye do shew the Lord's death till He come.

The congregation is then invited to come forward in an orderly fashion to receive the communion elements: first the bread, and then the cup. They are then to return to their seats with order.
Communion should end with a song of praise or a time of worship, all of which are invited to join in. The music can be pre-recorded, or live.

If foot-washing is to follow, it is performed at this time. The items for foot-washing should be distributed immediately after communion and people paired for the ordinance. The minister reads John 13:1-17 and concludes by saying, *As He did, do ye also.* All in the church wash one another's feet, with one sitting in a chair, and the other kneeling on the floor, using a basin of water and a towel.

COMMUNION DOS AND DON'TS:

- DO see communion as a union with Christ, with one another in the Body of Christ, and as a memorial of His death and resurrection.
- DO understand the relevance and importance of unity.
- DO teach on all aspects of communion, and the importance of communion.
- DO see communion as more than just a ceremony done a few times per year.
- DO hold communion at any event emphasizing unity, not just at an occasional Sunday service.
- DO uphold requirements to receive communion, and personal examination prior to receiving communion.
- DO have all appropriate items and elements ready and on hand for communion.
- DO use the correct elements for communion.
- DO take into account allergies to preservatives, such as sulfites (often present in grape juice), and abstinence from alcohol when selecting elements.
- DO preside over communion as a leader, and allow ministries of help to assist in the distribution of communion.
- DO dress appropriately for communion events.
- DO have a communion distribution plan.
- DO train ministry helps and workers in the plan for communion: preparation, distribution, and clean-up – as is relevant to the size and situation of the congregation.
- DO hold foot-washing services as part of communion, as often as is possible.

- DO advise people to dress appropriately for foot-washing events.

- DON'T alter communion elements out of convenience.
- DON'T approach communion as a "snack time" for the church.
- DON'T hold communion service without emphasizing the relevance of unity in belief and examination of conscience prior to distributing elements.
- DON'T let communion be handled as a haphazard event.
- DON'T hold a communion service without checking inventory, to make sure enough distribution materials and elements are available to all.
- DON'T act as a judge, refusing to distribute elements to certain people.
- DON'T forget about the importance of teaching and Scripture study on communion, unity, and foot-washing.
- DON'T allow inappropriate conduct during foot-washing.

SECTION IV

PRAYERS AND BLESSINGS OF THE CHURCH

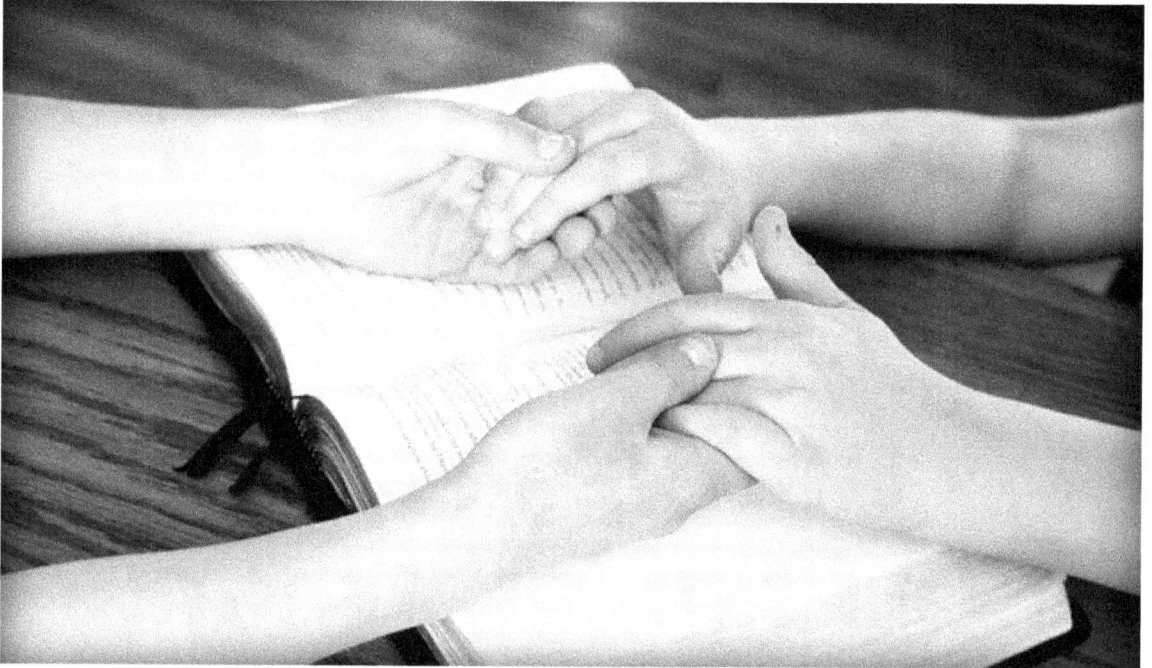

PRAYER

CHAPTER ELEVEN

PRAYERS

For God is my witness, Whom I serve with my [whole] spirit
[rendering priestly and spiritual service] in [preaching] the Gospel
and [telling] the good news of His Son, how incessantly I always mention
you when at my prayers.
- Romans 1:9 (AMPC)

I'VE added this section to our book on rites, rituals, and ordinances because, as leaders, we are often asked to pray in different circumstances…and we might have no idea what to say, especially when we are asked and we are not expecting to be asked to do anything. It often happens that we are asked to pray for something specific, in front of a group of people, and praying for that specific thing was not on our minds. Here, I want to inspire us to prayer. I have included 25 starter prayers on a diverse group of topics, many of which overlap with special ceremonies, rites, rituals, and ordinances we may either preside over or may assist with. At other times, they may be suitable for community services or other events where the opportunity to pray comes up, very unexpected. Instead of freezing up, use these prayers as needed and also allow them to inspire you to script your own prayers for topics that arise in various situations that require topical prayer. I encourage every minister to maintain a prayer book that records prayers of inspiration and meaning, and let this chapter start you on to thinking about the powerful way that prayers can transform, even when we keep them simple.

PRAYER FOR CHILDREN

Father,

We recognize there are so many things that can impact the lives of children and that many of these things can change the way they perceive the world as adults. We pray today for every child, that they may dwell in safety and security, and shall have their physical, emotional, and spiritual needs met. We pray that children who are unharmed shall remain unharmed. We pray for children who have been harmed by someone else to receive the healing and help they need. May all children come to know You.

In Jesus' Name we pray, amen.

PRAYER FOR COMMUNITIES IN TIMES OF TRAGEDY

Father,

We ask for Your mercy upon all of us when a community is hit with a terrible tragedy. People hurt, people take sides, people see injustice up front in their faces, and Lord, we pray that You would be with the communities that face tragedies. No matter the nature, they can bring terrible destruction on a city, town, or region. We pray for peace in the midst of tragedy. We pray that communities will come together under the banner of doing what is right and work together rather than working against each other. We believe that You can bring good out of bad, and transform what happens into something that causes all to examine themselves and become better people. Lord, be with Your people. Let us be forerunners in disaster and the first ones on the front lines to make a difference in our communities.

In Jesus' Name we pray, amen.

PRAYER FOR DIRECTION

Father,

Sometimes we just don't know the way to go, because the way is not clear to us. It's not always easy knowing where we should go, what we should do, and the path we should take. Lord, we ask that You would guide our steps and show us the way You would have us to go. We ask for Your protection and provision as we move in that way. Lord, help us to be led in a deeper way by the Holy Spirit. May we know and hear Your voice, and may You show us how to do all that You call us to do with wisdom and order.

In Jesus' Name we pray, amen.

PRAYER FOR ENDURANCE

Father,

When we grow weary and tired, we desire to give up and forget about the promises and visions You have placed within our lives. We have seen many wounded soldiers fall and never rise again, and we don't desire that to happen to us. Our desire is that we will experience the renewal needed to run our race to completion. Lord, we can't do this without You, so we ask You for the grace to endure. Help us win the battle, help us run the race. Let us know when we need to slow down or speed up. Let us know when to rest and when to step up our pace. In all things, guide and direct us.

In Jesus' Name we pray, amen.

PRAYER FOR FAMILY

Father,

You are the original parent of all of us, the guider, sustainer, and protector. It is through You that we learn about true love, looking at the work of the Father, the Son, and the Holy Spirit. Just as You are one, we, too, seek to be one. Help us to unite in our families through love. We pray for a love between members of families, for understanding and clarity. We know how hard relationships one to another can be, so we ask You to help us to see Your face in the relationships we have. We ask You to create peace where there is strife, love where there is hatred, and truth where there are lies. Show us how we can work out our differences and work together for You. I ask You to touch every member of my family, and bless their finances, their homes, meet their needs, and show each and every one of us a greater vision of You.

In Jesus' Name we pray, amen.

PRAYER OF GRACE BEFORE MEALS

Father,

We thank You for all good gifts that You have given to us, and right now we thank You for Your gift of food. May this meal nourish our bodies and may Your presence nourish our souls. From farm to table, may all who have been involved in this meal be blessed and kept. May those of us who share it with others be blessed by their company, and may we be kept in spiritual friendship as well as physical nourishment.

In Jesus' Name we pray, amen.

PRAYER FOR GOVERNMENT LEADERS

Father,

We often don't consider that being in leadership is a hard job and that we are commanded to pray for the leaders in positions of governmental power. Whether our leaders or the leaders of other nations, we pray for their wisdom and guidance in making right decisions. We pray leaders of every nations will consider the best interests of those they lead, and that the end of those decisions will be peace. We pray for leaders we agree with and we disagree with, and recognize that even though we may not agree with every decision someone makes, we respect they are in a difficult position of leadership and must use that office for the good of all involved. May we find greater ways to maintain Kingdom lives and live peaceably with all people.

In Jesus' Name we pray, amen.

PRAYER FOR THE GRIEVING

Father,

You know that the hurts and pains of this world seem endless. So many of Your people grieve, hurt by the losses and wounds of this world that seem unbearable. Send the Holy Spirit, the source of all comfort, to those who are hurting. Send us, as agents of Your love, to comfort those who grieve with compassion. Let us look for ways to encourage others, to help others out when they are having a bad time or are going through things that seem impossible to overcome, as agents of healing and wholeness. Let us be community, people who love by our actions and speak encouragement with our works. Send us, Lord. Don't just send anybody, send us.

In Jesus' Name we pray, amen.

PRAYER FOR HOLINESS AND INTEGRITY

Father,

Sometimes following You is hard, but we want to please You in all that we do. You have set us apart as a people unto You, and we stand upon our call as a chosen priesthood, a royal nation, a holy people. Guide us into our ways of integrity and show us how we can be truly set apart for You – not seeing to set ourselves apart by human means, but by being placed as a witness to Your glory and power. Guide us to do the right things in every situation, no matter who is present or who will know what we have done. If no one sees, Lord, we know that You do, and You are a faithful rewarder of those who do right.

In Jesus' Name we pray, amen.

PRAYER FOR HOPE

Father,

Our world often seems hopeless. We forget that You are Creator and that Your creation is, ultimately, Yours in the end. May we never look upon the things we see and feel helpless, because You have created us to do good and to make a difference. Where there is injustice, may we take action. Where there is fear, may we bring comfort. Where there is sadness, may we bring Your everlasting joy. Where there are problems, may we offer solutions. For every hopeless situation, may we bring Your hope. Let us never forget You are within us and You are among us, and that means we are never hopeless, nor are we ever alone. If we seek You, we shall always see hope.

In Jesus' Name we pray, amen.

PRAYER FOR THE INTERNATIONAL CHURCH

Father,

We know the church down here moves far beyond the immediacies we see in our own local churches and communities. We pray for Your insight to embrace the international communion of believers, wherever they may be. May You guide and protect each member of Your church, everywhere they go, and everywhere they set their foot to move. We pray for a greater sense of evangelism and unity among our international work. We pray that all people, everywhere, will lift up holy hands before You, praising and worshiping You in each language, among every tongue and tribe, everywhere in the world. We pray for freedom and understanding, that we can do all things through You, and we can come to an understanding of Your Word through the guidance of the Holy Spirit. May we raise up Christ, and Him crucified, and proclaim Him to a lost and dying world.

In Jesus' Name we pray, amen.

PRAYER TO KNOW GOD BETTER

Father,

It is our deepest desire to know You in a deeper way. We pray that as You would show Yourself to us, we would respond and follow You in kind. We seek to know You through Your Word, through Your Spirit, through Your Son, through Your gifts, through Your church, and through Your revelations to us. In our seeking, may we find You, and in our efforts to find You, may we come to know You.

In Jesus' Name we pray, amen.

PRAYER FOR LEADERS

Father,

We lift up our spiritual leaders to You because being a leader is hard. There are so many things leaders face as they confront the daily challenge to die to themselves and lift up Christ. With the struggles of life, Lord, let Your leaders be strong. May they guide people to You, and remember, this is not about them, themselves. May leaders find encouragement and refreshment in the spiritual things, in their relationship with You, Lord, and in their relationships with others. May each leader find their place in ministry, the place You have for them and the powerful anointing that will give them the grace to do what

You desire them to do.

In Jesus' Name we pray, amen.

PRAYER FOR A LOCAL CHURCH

Father,

We love being a part of Your church and we are blessed to be able to gather together in one accord and worship You through our local church. We ask that You would use us for Your glory. Give us the grace to lift Your Name high and to unify with our brothers and sisters, right here in our midst. Where there are divisions, we pray for greater unity. Let us work together for You. Let us open our doors so this city can find and discover You. May we never shut ourselves off to the concerns and needs of this area. Let us be a resource for good in our cities and show these people that they care. Lord, give us the grace to work with other churches in our area, always uniting with truth, and celebrating the work of fellowship that you seek to do within us.

In Jesus' Name we pray, amen.

PRAYER FOR LOVE, PEACE, AND FAITHFULNESS

Father,

The Word reveals to us many different values that we should embody in our lives. There are so many, we cannot list them all. Today we pray for the foundation of good values: love, peace, and faithfulness. If we love You and we love others, we will see peace reign in our lives. If we are faithful, we will be better people, who are easy to get along with and we will show forth Your excellence in all that we do. Your love, peace, and faithfulness in our lives will give us the grace to go the extra mile with our families, our friends, our churches, our communities, and our jobs. Through love, peace, and faithfulness, help us to be better parents, spouses, children, friends, citizens, church members, and leaders. Give us the grace to embody You in all that we do.

In Jesus' Name we pray, amen.

PRAYER FOR MISSIONS

Father,

We know the Word states that the harvest is great, but the workers are few. We pray for each and every missionary who sets their feet to follow You into known and unknown territory, that all might hear and believe the Gospel. It is our heart to stand and agree that Your missionaries will be provided open doors, open hearts, and full knowledge of movement and discernment when working in foreign territory for You. May we, the church, rise up in support of Your missionaries through our finances, our support, and our encouragement.

In Jesus' Name we pray, amen.

PRAYER FOR THE PERSECUTED

Father,

Many believers worldwide do not enjoy security as believers. They live with the threats of violence, terrorism, persecution, or death because they are believers in Christ. We lift these individuals up to You, Lord, and ask You to be with them. Let their lives stand as a witness to You, that they may speak to others about their faith through their conduct. May they have such a zeal for You that their oppressors are silenced, their witness is raised up, and others realize how important it is to live for You, just because they do what is right. May we remember them in our prayers, our lives, and our witness. May we have the fire for evangelism stirred within us because of the witness of the persecuted.

In Jesus' Name we pray, amen.

PRAYER FOR PROTECTION

Father,

> Sometimes we miss the mark and do not see things clearly, as we should. There are many spiritual forces we don't consider and there are many who work for various forces. This means not everything that is out there for our good, and that is why You have promised to protect us. We are not to fear, because You are on our side. As long as we keep with the plan and keep to Your path, we trust You will protect us. So, Father, protect us from every enemy, known and unknown. Protect us from false tongues, from false flattery, from deceit and deception. Protect us from physical, spiritual, mental, and emotional harm. Encourage us and guide us on Your way.

In Jesus' Name we pray, amen.

PRAYER FOR REFORMATION

Father,

> Too often we pray exclusively for revival without understanding that we need true reformation in our day and time. We do not just need mass conversion, but the ability to instruct and guide those who come forth because they have found You. We pray for the solidity of Christian schools and colleges; for seminaries and ministries that exist to instruct and educate on the Christian faith; and for congregations to emerge with educated leaders who know how to answer the hard questions of our faith. We pray for a rise in scholarship and an increased interest in spiritual education. We pray for those who are a part of new movement, new ideas, new concepts, new ways of looking at Your Word, that we are in desperate need of receiving. Above all,

we pray for hearts to turn to You like never before, seeing that You are good and you are all-knowing.

In Jesus' Name we pray, amen.

PRAYER FOR THE SICK

Father,

We thank You for always being with us and for recognizing the love Your people have for You. We know we can come before You and You will be faithful to receive us. Lord, Your servant (insert name) is hurting right now. They are experiencing the pain and trial of illness and desire Your touch to transform their lives. Lord, we stand and we believe that healing is from You and You alone, and that You can meet Your servant right where they are and bring about the healing that they need. Hear and answer our prayer for Your healing as we touch and agree.

In Jesus' Name we pray, amen.

PRAYER FOR THOSE IN NEED

Father,

So many in this world are hurting, hungry, impoverished, without work, lonely, sick, unhappy, or otherwise afflicted. Many are just getting by, feeling like they are missing something in life because it is hard for them to make ends meet. The needs that these people have are great, and we ask that You would send people to meet the needs of these individuals, set straight from heaven to them. Stir within us, Lord, the desire to help others who are in need and not wait for someone else to do what needs doing. Give us hands of hope, hearts of compassion, prepared focus and vision, so we can make Your Kingdom come brighter and better than it ever has been. It takes all of us, Lord, so as we pray for others to meet needs, we pray that we shall be equipped to meet them, as well. Let us never forget those in need, remembering them in our prayers and our good thoughts, encouraging others with our actions as much as our words. May those in need feel Your presence and know that others care about them.

In Jesus' Name we pray, amen.

PRAYER FOR TRAVEL

Father,

We know that whenever we venture beyond the comfortable regions, we take a risk. We pray that in our travel, we shall always find a greater sense of Your presence and Your work all around us, because know that if we do not venture, we will not gain. Guide our steps, Lord. Protect us in travel from the seen and unseen that we fail to consider. Keep us safe and return us home, that our travels may be a testimony unto You.

In Jesus' Name we pray, amen.

PRAYER FOR UNITY

Father,

You teach us about love and about relationship. The unity of the Father, the Son, and the Holy Spirit shows us about being one, about blessing others, and about working with others. Lord, Your call for us to be one does not mean we all must be the same. Help us to embrace and receive the "different" among us. We ask Your grace to help us work out our differences and our misunderstandings, as we know those are not things we can work out ourselves, by our own power. We humbly request You to show us truth, as Your Word is truth, and the Spirit shall lead us into all truth. Help us to put our flesh aside and allow others to be themselves, confirming they have the right to their opinions and that unified opinions are not required for spiritual unity. Give us a heart, a mind, and a vision for the things You desire us to have. Let us be Kingdom-minded, focused beyond this world and the things that divide us. As we come to a greater understanding of Your love, let us show it through our unity.

In Jesus' Name we pray, amen.

PRAYER FOR AN UNSAVED PERSON

Father,

We believe in the power of prayer and the power of change. We know that we come to You as You have drawn us, and we believe today on behalf of (insert name) who needs to know You. Through Your lovingkindness, draw (insert name) to you. Let them see You in grace and power, and know You are a good God, a good and loving Father, a rewarder of those who seek You. Show yourself to them, that they might seek Your face, in truth, and live.

In Jesus' Name we pray, amen.

PRAYER FOR WISDOM AND SPIRITUAL GROWTH

Father,

We know we can't live this life and gain spiritual insights without wisdom. We ask that You would bless us with Your wisdom, with insights that only You can give us. Show us the end before we get there, and reveal Yourself to us in all things. We know we need You and that You are the source of all wisdom. As we grow in wisdom, may we grow in spirit, as well. May our spiritual growth take us to deeper places in You and reveal where we can do better, where we need to surrender more of our lives to You, and how we can better develop spiritual discipline in our lives.

In Jesus' Name we pray, amen.

RECEIVING FROM GOD

CHAPTER TWELVE

BLESSINGS

*Jabez cried to the God of Israel, saying, Oh, that You would bless me
and enlarge my border, and that Your hand might be with me,
and You would keep me from evil so it might not hurt me!
And God granted his request.
- 1 Chronicles 4:10 (AMPC)*

I never thought much about the principle of blessings until people started asking me to "bless them" or to "pray that God would bless them." The truth is that Scripture is full of blessings and there are many ways that we can expand upon the blessings of Scripture to make them our own and encourage others with them through the work that we do in ministry. Sometimes we don't take the time to consider the blessing work of Scripture and to see God's incredible hand of blessing present in the Scriptures, there to bless and keep us in all sorts of circumstances. The blessings in this chapter, are all found in Scripture, and are perfect for introductions or dismissals, special occasions or services, and fit most, if not all, instances where blessings may be required.

GENESIS 27:28-29

Therefore God give thee of the dew of heaven, and the fatness of the earth, and plenty of corn and wine:

Let people serve thee, and nations bow down to thee: be lord over thy brethren, and let thy mother's sons bow down to thee: cursed be every one that curseth thee, and blessed be he that blesseth thee.

NUMBERS 6:24-26

The LORD bless thee, and keep thee:
    The LORD make His face shine upon thee, and be gracious unto thee:
    The LORD lift up His countenance upon thee, and give thee peace.

DEUTERONOMY 30:16

In that I command thee this day to love the LORD thy God, to walk in His ways, and to keep His commandments and His statutes and His judgments, that thou mayest live and multiply: and the LORD thy God shall bless thee in the land whither thou goest to possess it.

PSALM 1:1-3

Blessed is the man that walketh not in the counsel of the ungodly, nor standeth in the way of sinners, nor sitteth in the seat of the scornful.

But his delight is in the law of the LORD; and in His law doth he meditate day and night.

And he shall be like a tree planted by the rivers of water, that bringeth forth his fruit in his season; his leaf also shall not wither; and whatsoever he doeth shall prosper.

JEREMIAH 17:7-8

Blessed is the man that trusteth in the LORD, and whose hope the LORD is.

For he shall be as a tree planted by the waters, and that spreadeth out her roots by the river, and shall not see when heat cometh, but her leaf shall be green; and shall not be careful in the year of drought, neither shall cease from yielding fruit.

PSALM 20:4-5

Grant thee according to Thine own heart, and fulfil all Thy counsel.

We will rejoice in Thy salvation, and in the Name of our God we will set up our banners: the LORD fulfil all thy petitions.

PSALM 67:1-7

God be merciful unto us, and bless us; and cause His face to shine upon us; Selah.

That Thy way may be known upon earth, thy saving health among all nations.

Let the people praise Thee, O God; let all the people praise Thee.

O let the nations be glad and sing for joy: for Thou shalt judge the people righteously, and govern the nations upon earth. Selah.

Let the people praise Thee, O God; let all the people praise Thee.

Then shall the earth yield her increase; and God, even our own God, shall bless us.

God shall bless us; and all the ends of the earth shall fear Him.

PROVERBS 16:3

Commit Thy works unto the LORD, and thy thoughts shall be established.

MATTHEW 5:3-12

Blessed are the poor in spirit: for theirs is the kingdom of heaven.

Blessed are they that mourn: for they shall be comforted.

Blessed are the meek: for they shall inherit the earth.

Blessed are they which do hunger and thirst after righteousness: for they shall be filled.

Blessed are the merciful: for they shall obtain mercy.

Blessed are the pure in heart: for they shall see God.

Blessed are the peacemakers: for they shall be called the children of God.

Blessed are they which are persecuted for righteousness' sake: for theirs is the kingdom of heaven.

Blessed are ye, when men shall revile you, and persecute you, and shall say all manner of evil against you falsely, for My sake.

Rejoice, and be exceeding glad: for great is your reward in heaven: for so persecuted they the prophets which were before you.

EPHESIANS 1:2-6

Blessed be the God and Father of our Lord Jesus Christ, Who hath blessed us with all spiritual blessings in heavenly places in Christ:

According as He hath chosen us in Him before the foundation of the world, that we should be holy and without blame before Him in love:

Having predestinated us unto the adoption of children by Jesus Christ to Himself, according to the good pleasure of His will,

To the praise of the glory of His grace, wherein He hath made us accepted in the beloved.

PHILIPPIANS 4:4-9

Rejoice in the Lord always: and again I say, Rejoice.

Let your moderation be known unto all men. The Lord is at hand.

Be careful for nothing; but in every thing by prayer and supplication with thanksgiving let your requests be made known unto God.

And the peace of God, which passeth all understanding, shall keep your hearts and minds through Christ Jesus.

Finally, brethren, whatsoever things are true, whatsoever things are honest, whatsoever things are just, whatsoever things are pure, whatsoever things are lovely, whatsoever things are of good report; if there be any virtue, and if there be any praise, think on these things.

Those things, which ye have both learned, and received, and heard, and seen in me, do: and the God of peace shall be with you.

PHILIPPIANS 4:23

The grace of our Lord Jesus Christ be with you all. Amen.

PHILEMON 1:25

The grace of our Lord Jesus Christ be with your spirit. Amen.

3 JOHN 1:2

Beloved, I wish above all things that thou mayest prosper and be in health, even as thy soul prospereth.

JUDE 1:2

Mercy unto you, and peace, and love, be multiplied.

REVELATION 22:20-21

He which testifieth these things saith, Surely I come quickly. Amen. Even so, come, Lord Jesus.

The grace of our Lord Jesus Christ be with you all. Amen.

COURSE ASSIGNMENTS

Project List

1) Write an editorial essay (3-6 sentences minimum) about the sacred in ministry and in the church. Where do you think it is missing? How do you think rites, rituals, and ordinances help restore the sacred in the church today? Why is the sacred a part of God's Kingdom?

2) Write one essay (3-6 sentences minimum) on the relevance and importance of each rite, ritual, and ordinance presented below (nine essays in total):
   a. Ordination
   b. Appointment
   c. Weddings
   d. Funerals
   e. Graduation Services and Sacred Assemblies
   f. Presentations/Dedications
   g. Consecration
   h. Anointing
   i. Water Baptism
   j. Holy Communion

3) As a leader, write an essay (3-6 sentences minimum) on how you would prepare an individual for each of the following rites (three essays in total)
    a. Ordination
    b. Consecration
    c. Water Baptism

4) In essay format (3-6 sentences minimum) explain the difference between ministry ordination and appointments.

5) As a leader, prepare a graduation service and a sacred assembly.

6) As a leader, write out the instructional steps you would provide to prepare helps ministry train for communion service and anointing service.

7) Provide a general outline for wedding counseling and preparation and funeral preparation.

8) As a leader, write an essay (3-6 sentences minimum) on how you would handle an anointing service.

9) Select two rites, rituals, or ordinances and write out what you, as a leader, would do, from start to finish. Include the following:
    a. Planning
    b. Preparation for both the individuals and the ministers involved
    c. Teaching on the rite, ritual, or ordinance at hand
    d. Presentation for the minister
    e. The rite, ritual, or ordinance itself

REFERENCES

REFERENCE LIST

[1]Basic information referenced from "Wedding Ceremony Traditions" by Elaine Walker, http://elainewalker.suite101.com/wedding-ceremony-traditions-a56527. Accessed April 2012.

[2]Ibid.

[3]Ibid.

[4]From *The Manual of Discipline* as is found in Willis Barnstone's *The Other Bible: Ancient Alternative Scriptures.* San Francisco, California: HarperCollins San Francisco, 1984.

[5]No longer in print.

ABOUT THE AUTHOR

Dr. Lee Ann B. Marino, Ph.D., D.Min., D.D.

Dr. Lee Ann B. Marino, Ph.D., D.Min., D.D. is an apostle, missionary, apostolic theologian, Bible scholar, women's advocate, feminist, activist, university chancellor, songwriter, worship leader, worship dancer, and Senior Prelate, founder, and visionary for Apostolic Fellowship International Revival Ministries (AFIRM). In acknowledgement of her extensive work in the apostolic, she has been called "the greatest apostle in the modern church." A seminary doctoral graduate of Apostolic Preachers College (now Apostolic University) in Philosophy, Theology, Divinity, and Religion/Comparative Religion, Dr. Marino's approach to preaching, teaching, Spiritual matters, and Scriptural education have touched a generation looking for leadership, connection, and understanding in our modern times.

In nearly two decades of ministry, Dr. Marino has made the joke that she's been "every Pentecostal denomination under the sun." A college exploration of religion back in 1997 led her to "get saved the first time," immersing her into a spiritual world of gifts, devotional spirituality, and an intense call to ministry, sometimes in churches that worked – and sometimes in settings that went seriously awry. Through a series of different events, including periods of time in Charismatic, Holiness, Full Gospel, Oneness, Apostolic, and non-denominational, Dr. Marino found her own calling – and her own ministerial identity – in neo-Apostolic, a division of modern Pentecostal understanding that respects and heralds the ancestry of the past, along with vision for the modern-day issues and circumstances the church and the world face today.

Dr. Marino has been in ministry since 1998 and founded Apostolic Fellowship International Ministries (now Apostolic Fellowship International Revival Ministries_ in 2004. She was ordained as a pastor in 2002 and as an apostle in 2010. Her experiences have taken her to over five hundred religious services and experiences of all sorts throughout the years, both Christian and non-Christian alike, as she studied and strived to learn what all believe. The work of Apostolic Fellowship International Revival Ministries now extends to all Christian borders, working in different Protestant and non-denominational churches alike. Apostle's vision is about the church now, honoring history while looking forward, and about becoming "all things to all people," that some may be saved. Her fellowship encompasses twenty churches and ministries worldwide, thousands of friends, and includes the work of Sanctuary International Fellowship Tabernacle – SIFT, a church movement dedicated to leading people to God without politics, where she emphasizes relationship, acceptance, experience, and service. In covering, her emphasis is on the unique development of each leader to become all God has for them to be in their specific gifting and ministries. She has preached and taught throughout the United States, Puerto Rico, and in Europe. Affectionately nicknamed "the Spitfire," she is best-known for her work in the apostolic, her instruction for church leaders and ministers, her work in the study of gender, sexual ethics, and human sexuality, and her work in women's ministry through the study of Female Apologetics, established and first taught by Dr. Marino herself. She has spent over twenty years in advocacy, education, and work for and with minority communities, including women, African-Americans, Latinos, and the LGBT community.

Her work is not without acclaim, and she is the recipient of several awards and has been featured in many magazine publications and on many radio and television programs over the years, including Woman of the Year 2012 and Mother of the Year 2013. As Chancellor of Apostolic

University since 2004, her teachings in the apostolic, church history and protocol, Scripture studies, textbooks, and educational materials on many issues of faith, ethics, gender, sociology, church history, theology, and philosophy have reached individuals in over seventy-five countries. Having written over twenty-five books, including her best-sellers, *Ministry School Boot Camp: Training For Helps Ministries, Appointments, And Beyond* (Righteous Pen Publications, 2014), *Awakening Christian Ministry: The Call To Serve Others As We Serve Jesus Christ* (Righteous Pen Publications, 2014), *Stumbling To Nineveh: A Journey Through The Book Of Jonah* (Righteous Pen Publications, 2015); *Discovering Intimacy: A Journey Through The Song Of Solomon* (Righteous Pen Publications, 2015); and *Ministering To LGBTs – And Those Who Love Them* (Apostolic University Press, 2016).

Dr. Marino is editor-in-chief of *Kingdom Now* Magazine and host of the *Kingdom Now* television and radio programs, as well as CEO and designer for Rose of Sharon Creations, CEO of Righteous Pen Media, and Editor-in-Chief for The Righteous Pen Publications Group. She is also a member of the Women's Christian Temperance Union, a historical women's organization with long-held ties to women's rights, ordination, and ministry. Her main website is www.kingdompowernow.org.